THE PENGUIN POETS

D46

CANADIAN VERSE

The Penguin Book of CANADIAN VERSE

Revised Edition

EDITED WITH AN

INTRODUCTION AND NOTES BY

Ralph Gustafson

PENGUIN BOOKS

Penguin Books Ltd, Harmondsworth, Middlesex, England
Penguin Books Inc., 3300 Clipper Mill Road, Baltimore, Md 21211, U.S.A.
Penguin Books Australia Ltd, Ringwood, Victoria, Australia

—

First published 1958
Revised edition 1967

—

—

Made and printed in Great Britain by
Cox & Wyman Ltd, London, Reading and Fakenham
Set in Monotype Fournier

To the memory of

E. J. PRATT

Contents

CONTENTS

CONTENTS

Acknowledgements

PERMISSION to use copyright material is gratefully acknowledged to the following:

Behrman House, Inc., New York for 'Heirloom' and 'The Still Small Voice' from *Hath not a Jew . . .* by A. M. Klein.

Chatto & Windus Ltd, London, for the poems from *The Wounded Prince* and *The Net and the Sword* by Douglas Le Pan; and Lyric XCIII from *Sappho, One Hundred Lyrics* by Bliss Carman.

Dodd, Mead & Company Inc., New York, for 'Low Tide on Grand Pré', 'A Northern Vigil', 'A Seamark', and 'Christmas Song', by Bliss Carman, reprinted by permission of Dodd, Mead & Company from *Bliss Carman's Poems.*

Estate of Frederick George Scott for the poems by Frederick George Scott.

Faber and Faber Limited, London, for the two poems from *Friday's Child* by Wilfred Watson.

Farrar, Straus & Cudahy, Inc., New York, for the two poems from *Friday's Child* by Wilfred Watson, copyright 1955 by Wilfred Watson, published by Farrar, Straus & Cudahy, Inc.

Jewish Publication Society of America, Philadelphia, for 'Psalms VI and XII' from *Poems* by A. M. Klein.

Alfred A. Knopf, Inc., New York, for the poems of E. J. Pratt, reprinted from *Collected Poems*, copyright 1945 by Edward J. Pratt.

McClelland & Stewart Limited, Toronto, for 'My Bird-Wrung Youth' from *The Colour as Naked* by Patrick Anderson; 'Shrouds and Away' from *Border River* by A. G. Bailey; selections from *Selected Poems* by Earle Birney; selections from *Bliss Carman's Poems*; selections from *The Spice-Box of Earth* and *Flowers for Hitler* by Leonard Cohen; sonnets from *Deeper into the Forest* and *The Chequered Shade* by Roy Daniells; 'Jardin de la Chapelle Expiatoire' from *The Strength of the Hills* by Robert Finch; 'Utrillo's World' from *The Deficit Made Flesh* by John Glassco; selections from *Rivers among Rocks* and *Sift in an Hourglass* by Ralph Gustafson; selections from *Collected Poems* by Irving Layton; 'Summer' from *The Metal and the Flower* by P. K. Page; selections from *The Complete Poems of Marjorie Pickthall*; 'At Delos' from *The Circle of Affection* by Duncan Campbell Scott.

The Macmillan Company of Canada Limited, Toronto, for 'Admonition for Spring', 'Now There Is Nothing Left', and 'Look, I Have Thrown All Right' from *The Ill-Tempered Lover* by L. A. MacKay: selection from *A Suit of Nettles* by James Reaney; selections from *Collected Poems* by E. J. Pratt; 'Lens' and 'In June and Gentle Oven' from *The Hangman Ties the Holly* by Anne Wilkinson. 'A Cautionary Tale' and excerpts from 'Nature Be Damned' reprinted by permission of the estate of Anne Wilkinson and The Macmillan Company of Canada Limited.

Michigan State University Press for 'Ode: On the Death of William

Butler Yeats', 'The Plot against Proteus' and 'The Archer' from *A Sort of Ecstasy* by A. J. M. Smith.

The New Yorker Magazine, Inc., for 'War on the Periphery' by George Johnston, Corp. © 1951 The New Yorker Magazine, Inc.

W. W. Norton & Company Inc., New York, for '. . . Person, or A Hymn on and to the Holy Ghost', 'For Dr and Mrs Dresser', and 'Janitor Working on Threshold' from *The Dumbfounding* by Margaret Avison © 1966 by Margaret Avison.

Oxford University Press, Toronto, for 'The Statue' from *Poems* by Robert Finch; 'Quebec Farmhouse' and 'Brummell at Calais' from *A Point of Sky* by John Glassco; 'Music in the Air' from *Home Free* by George Johnston; 'The Swan' and 'The Fisherman' from *The Boatman* by Jay Macpherson; '*On Knowing* Nothing', 'News of the Phoenix' and 'The Sorcerer' from *Collected Poems* by A. J. M. Smith.

L. C. Page & Company, Boston for selections from *Poems* by Charles G. D. Roberts; and 'Lyric XCIII' from *Sappho* by Bliss Carman: reprinted by permission of the copyright owner, L. C. Page & Company, Boston.

Proprietors of *Punch* for 'In Flanders Fields' by John McCrae, reproduced by permission of *Punch*.

The Ryerson Press, Toronto, for 'Cold Colloquy' from *The White Centre* by Patrick Anderson; 'Bushed' from *Trial of a City* by Earle Birney; 'How One Winter Came in the Lake Region' from *The Collected Poems of Wilfred Campbell*; 'The Pomegranate' from *The Searching Image* by Louis Dudek; 'Roadside near Moscow' from *A Window on the North* by R. A. D. Ford; 'Haying' from *Marshlands* by John Frederic Herebin; 'The Rocking Chair' and 'Bread' from *The Rocking Chair* by A. M. Klein; selections from *Collected Poems of Raymond Knister*; two sonnets from *By Stubborn Stars* by Kenneth Leslie; 'The Thing is Violent' from *A Breakfast for Barbarians* by Gwendolyn MacEwen; 'Zalinka' from *Complete Poems of Tom MacInnes*; 'David' from *Black and Secret Man* by Eli Mandel; 'The Anatomy of Angels' from *Under the Ice* by Alden Nowlan; 'At Robin Lake' from *The Crafte so Longe to Lerne* by Alfred Purdy; selections from *Selected Poems of Sir Charles G. D. Roberts*; 'The Blue Heron' and 'The Wreckers' Prayer' from *The Leather Bottle* by Theodore Goodridge Roberts; 'The Piper of Arll', 'Thoughts', 'Watkwenies', 'The Onondaga Madonna', 'The Sailor's Sweetheart', 'A Song' from *The Selected Poems of Duncan Campbell Scott*; 'A Grain of Rice', 'Caring', 'Bonne Entente' from *Events and Signals* by F. R. Scott; 'The Yak' and 'Exile' from *Leaves in the Wind* by Virna Sheard; 'Ode: On the Death of William Butler Yeats', 'The Plot against Proteus', 'The Archer' from *A Sort of Ecstasy* by A. J. M. Smith; 'The Six-quart Basket' and 'Where the Blue Horses' from *The Colour of the Times* by Raymond Souster; 'Thou Didst Say Me' from *The Second Silence* and 'The Season's Lovers' from *The Season's Lovers* by Miriam Waddington.

The University of New Brunswick for permission for world rights outside Canada and U.S.A. to reprint the selections from the poems of Bliss Carman.

ACKNOWLEDGEMENTS

Mrs B. H. Warr for the poems by Bertram Warr.

University of Toronto Press for 'Northern Water Thrush', 'Poem for Good Friday' and 'Boy in the Lamont Poetry Room, Harvard' from *The Sun is Axeman* by D. G. Jones.

Grateful acknowledgement is made to the following authors: Patrick Anderson for 'Drinker' from *A Tent for April* (First Statement Press); Margaret Avison for her poems; George Bowering for his poems from *The Silver Wire* (Contact Press); John Robert Colombo for his poems; Pierre Coupey for his poem from *Bring Forth the Cowards* (McGill Poetry Series); Louis Dudek for 'Dawn' from *Twenty Four Poems*, selections from *Europe*, 'The Jungle' and 'Mouths' from *The Transparent Sea* (Contact Press); R. G. Everson for 'Child with Shell' and 'When I'm Going Well' from *A Lattice for Momos* (Contact Press) and 'Rogue Pearunners' from *Wrestle with an Angel* (Delta Canada); R. A. D. Ford for 'The Thieves of Love'; Eldon Grier for 'Quebec' from *A Morning from Scraps*, 'In Memory of Garcia Lorca' from *Poems*, 'On the Subject of Waves' and 'View from a Window' from *A Friction of Lights* (Contact Press); Daryl Hine for his poem from *The Carnal and the Crane*, McGill Poetry series; George Jonas for 'Five Stanzas on Perfection' from *New Wave Canada* (Contact Press); D. G. Jones for 'Annunciation'; Lionel Kearns for 'In-Group' and 'Insight'; Leo Kennedy for his poems; Irving Layton for his poems from *The Improved Binoculars*; Dorothy Livesay for selections from *The Colour of God's Face*; Malcolm Lowry for his poems; L. A. MacKay for 'Propertian'; Jay Macpherson for 'The Woods No More'; Eli Mandel for 'Job' from *Trio*, 'Phaeton' and 'Merits of Laughter and Lust' from *Fuseli Poems* (Contact Press); Tom Marshall for 'Astrology' from *The Beast with Three Backs* (Quarry Press); John Newlove for 'I Talk to You' and 'Good Company, Fine Houses' from *Moving in Alone* (Contact Press); Alden Nowlan for 'God Sour the Milk of the Knacking Wench' from *Wind in a Rocky Country* (Emblem Book), 'The Execution' from *The Things Which Are* (Contact Press), and for 'Beets'; Michael Ondaatje for his poem; Alfred Purdy for 'Wilderness Gothic' and 'The Sculptors'; P. K. Page for poems from *As Ten as Twenty*; W. W. E. Ross for his poems; F. R. Scott for 'Calamity'; Kay Smith for her poem from *Footnote to the Lord's Prayer* (First Statement Press); Raymond Souster for 'The Day before Christmas', and for 'Flight of the Roller-Coaster' from *The Selected Poems* (Contact Press); Miriam Waddington for 'Green World Two'; Phyllis Webb for 'Rilke'.

Diligent inquiry has been made to establish the owners of copyright material; if anyone has been overlooked, the editor makes sincere apologies.

Introduction

CANADIAN poetry has had self-respect and integrity from the first. One assumes that any poetry has. But the assertion is well made in connexion with Canadian poetry. There is a prevailing ignorance that supposes the opposite. The prejudice exists largely in the opinion that Canadian poetry is a feeble and pale reflection of the British poetic scene, that it is, in its later manifestation, obedient to American poetic activity and conveniently supplanted by it. The present anthology offers a hundred years of Canadian poetry. It is a poetry of distinction.

The poet cannot be asked to find his national identity before the factors that present it to him exist. Canadian poets identifiable as such, have had to wait for Canada. Canadian poetry came to maturity slowly and with difficulty. Slowly, since the making of a Canadian existence was late and vast; with difficulty, since the population which could support a culture was meagre and because the urgent preoccupation with commerce and industry vitiated its values. The stifling of the creative arts stifled self-recognition. Canadian poetry existed by virtue of its own integrity.

Meanwhile, in the sense of the handing down of an ethos, two traditions, the British and the French, were viable. English-Canadian writers wrote naturally in the belief that they were a part of the heritage that includes the author of *Beowulf* and Chaucer. They still do. Tradition in the sense of formal ceremonies, cricket instead of lacrosse, Canadians began diverging from long ago. To the first poet in this book, such credentials were no longer necessary.

The confusion that to recognize a tradition as natural is an imitation, has led a number of critics into a great deal of waste motion. They are afraid that this is colonial-mindedness, Canadian poetry the likeness of the poor British relation that rather disgracefully but happily left for the colonies. There is much poetry in Canada that fits the picture. It is all bad poetry. Why deal with it? The assumption by good Canadian poets that the British spiritual heritage was natural to them is another matter. It upsets high-strung patriotic critics. Early Canadian poets, born abroad, were nostalgic. Canada was a wild and big place. There is a great deal in their poems of Do the bourns of the glens still waggle. They wanted to know. But they also looked around them. None of them in this book is colonial-minded. The earlier poets were sensitive that they were not a nation of achieved greatness, they therefore sometimes exhort in a parochial and non-poetic manner. This is left-hand evidence they are not colonial-minded. They liked what they saw. They accepted what was not an affectation. The British tradition of justice is satisfactory to Canadians. So is Wordsworth's way of looking at a daffodil – the daffodil grows in Canada. Canada did not hunt nightingales. The tomato is not the tomayto. In the United States, that is very British. The Canadians think nothing of it and eat it, very often, with sugar, which is very unBritish.

The fact that nineteenth-century Canadian poets wrote in the manner of the nineteenth century, has bothered the critics. They let the imitators upset them. Valid Canadian poets, immigrant or native born, started where they had to: with the traditions of imaginative attack and the conventions of technique of their immediate predecessors or contemporaries elsewhere. There is in these valid poets a great deal that is imitative, that is not even emulative. Keats, Tennyson, Arnold, and Emerson were overwhelming. But they had tough personalities, these early Canadian poets, and they looked where they wanted to. In scathing verse Isabella Valancy Crawford looked into General Wolseley's war on the Zulus under Cetewayo; Isabella Valancy Crawford was a young woman living in obscurity in Toronto. She also almost made a myth out of the forests and weather of wild Ontario. She wrote a neo-Classic narrative poem. Charles G. D. Roberts wrote another. It was being done. Their samples can compare with any. Lampman wrote sonnets like any of his contemporaries, they are as good and better; untransplantable sonnets that cannot be mistaken as other than Canadian. Neither can Roberts's. Charles Sangster wrote of the St Lawrence and Saguenay rivers in Spenserian stanzas. The rivers cannot be mistaken for the Thames or the Concord. Heavysege in 1850 was trudging around Montreal with an Elizabethan play in his imagination, the most spirited since Elizabeth. Stratford on the Ontario Avon should read it.

Canadian poetry divides roughly into three main periods; each has the same integrity, the same skilful moderation that is aware of the continuity of its heritage, a recalcitrance of personality; the last period, the cumulative identity that is Canadian.

The earliest verses written in Canada are lively and loyal, but none is to be found in this book. There are some nice turns of wit and satire, there are some vivid lines on early Canadian settler life, but the poetry is unexceptional. The substantial beginning was made by the Three Charleses – Heavysege, Sangster, and Mair. Heavysege is a considerable poet. His major work is a closet drama, *Saul.* The hero struggles aginst his destiny without having made it, the drama is without the conditions for tragedy. Much of the writing is transcription. But when Heavysege gets away from his Biblical texts, the drama takes on a power that is impressive.

> Boy, blow, and let
> Thy full heart leap into thine instrument,
> And dance for joy a measure: in thy horn
> Thou wilt not stumble o'er the stony dead.

> Ha, ha!
> Those were the days of frolic! Malzah laughed
> For a whole century afterward.

> I've long been sad: 't is time a cock should crow
> When morning breaks.

> Now let me die, for I indeed was slain
> With my three sons.

Heavysege touches mastery. In his later play, *Count Filippo*, he felt compelled to be moral – the comic richness ends up in a flat conventional field-day of penitence – but for sheer exuberance, liveliness, and linguistics, North America has little to equal it.

Charles Sangster states quite simply, 'I love my art'. The strength, in a few poems, is felt. One is in humble touch with a man whose meeting of tragedy, the death of one he loved, is pure and sincere, and whose sincerity and purity were at one time mocked. He loved crashing thunderstorms and uncomplicated morality. He is all innocence.

> The moon, like to a royal traveller,
> Her silver chariot axle-deep in stars,
> Rides the burning labyrinth of worlds.

Charles Mair's most considerable production, the drama *Tecumseh*, fails in character and cohesion, but the blank verse rises at times to a fluent unadorned line that powerfully carries the history. He had a burning love of Canada, and when he wrote of the details of homes and nature around him, achieved a fine effect.

With the Group of the Sixties – poets born near the Confederation of 1867 who came to their maturity in the 1890s: Roberts, Lampman, Carman, Duncan Campbell Scott – Canada gained poets who were national. A Canadian literature was being created. Each of this group wrote fluently and well, often exceedingly well. There was technical excellence, a less innocent national awareness, definition of nature and locality, a compassion and virility, and a united dedication to the art of poetry. Canada could not be, after them, careless of her culture.

There is much inferior work in the Group of the Sixties, they were prolific poets. Roberts overstrains his Emersonian striving toward a cosmic consciousness; Lampman is a poet of one theme; Carman, largely, is at his worst in the poems which present themselves as his best, when he is capturing the 'oversoul' and is down the lanes as a fine vagabond; Tom MacInnes, another poet of this Group, wrote arbitrarily; Duncan Campbell Scott, perhaps too occasionally. Each can be run back obviously to Keats, Shelley, Tennyson, Arnold, Emerson.

But the scholarly pursuit of derivation is a game for 'the blind bookworm', as Lampman has him. 'The feeling of delight is the thing, not its cause', says Duncan Campbell Scott. And if the adverse criticism is placed here, it is to safeguard the statement that these poets are each, in his scope, as distinguished poets as North America has produced. In his earlier poetry – where Roberts is rooted to his Tantramar – and in certain of his later poems wherein the New Brunswick scene is revisited, Roberts is at his most impressive; in his sensitive evocation of the rural scene, his depth of imagination, his fine ear, and humble nobility of spirit. Lampman is supreme in his great subject, the landscape – the landscape of Ontario – the natural beauty of the world and the sorrow and loneliness of man who inhabits it. He is a master of the sonnet. In Carman's best is a clear, beautiful music, an honesty that is the daring of innocence, and over all, a joyousness of spirit and a gentleness of soul that are heedlessly winning – an imagination which Lampman found 'that of our own northern land'. The poetry of Duncan Campbell Scott is of a man who loved life wholly, affectionately, and at all times; where the word in Lampman is dream, the word in Duncan Campbell Scott is memory; he is a technician of refinement. In 'The Piper of Arll' he has written one of the few successful poems of poetry as music – a ballad of the fatal possession by the world of the beauty which longs to be one with it. MacInnes was himself as much as he could be; wrote of his belles dames sans merci, but thanked them and moved on to other damozels; the word, in MacInnes, is charity.

They were long-lived poets. Lampman apart, all but the youngest of today's poets could have known them. They were in the romantic tradition. One or two good poets, like Marjorie Pickthall, lingered in a sort of purple afterglow; but Romanticism was done. The majority belonging to the span of years before the century got well started, trying to write out the romantic tradition, were, or are, too late.

Striding the breach of accomplishment to new accomplishment is a redoubtable poet, E. J. Pratt. A master narrator, a technician of splendour and man of compassion and ironic depth, Pratt is one of the outstanding figures of Canadian writing. The pace, scope, dauntlessness, and comedy – Canada is everywhere in him. Suddenly, someone was writing:

> A bull moose that had died from gas
> While eating toadstools near Ungava.

The thrust of personality onto the poetic scene was grand. The sweep and buckle of obstructive satire entered Canadian verse; a sense of comedy burbled the Pierian springs; machines were admitted; a narrative irony was existent. E. J. Pratt is a poet of heroic proportions, not an epic poet, but epic in scope; not a tragic poet, but a poet with a profound sense of tragedy. Canada was being defined. In 1928, W. W. E. Ross's 'northern' poems were written, setting forth precisely, with wonder and freshness, and in verse that broke away from the old conventions, the changing qualities of Canada's natural scene. Raymond Knister was writing his poems of rural Ontario.

The publication in 1936 of a slim anthology called *New Provinces*, presenting the work of Finch, Kennedy, Klein, Pratt, F. R. Scott, and A. J. M. Smith, dispelled any illusion that the methods of thought and technique that had prevailed, stretching back from the Georgians to the nineteenth-century romanticism, were adequate to express the contemporary scene; trips to the Canadian fields and streams in a wondrous frame of mind would no longer do. The literary techniques, the advances of Yeats and Eliot, were assimilated by the *New Provinces* poets; wit came in, science, satire, and precision. An immediate social context was made essential.

In the 1940s, there was an invigoration. Protest – social, environmental, personal, economic – was strenuously voiced. The First World War had shaken individual faiths and beliefs. The Second World War smashed values wholesale. Personality, for its survival, was thrown on toughness of character. Canadian poets showed it. The Canadian poets of the forties demanded dignity, personal and social, buttressed it, defended it, and published it. With angry conviction, they stuck to values, like love, uncommercialized Christmas, unconformity, time not speed; they resented the stapled forms of Life, Peek, and Digest. Layton identified himself with the truth that the natural man is a creation of nobility, Dudek and Souster were a proof that spiritual toughness is compassion. Earle Birney, Klein, F. R. Scott, A. J. M. Smith, wrote with continuing force of the times and the desperate need of the times.

They are still writing of the condition of man, they are writing as well as any of their contemporaries in England and the United States. They are accomplished technically. Their phrasing is Canadian. It is becoming increasingly apparent that Canada has a poetry that is distinctly her own.

What is Canadian? The specifics of contemporary Canadian poetry are these:

The sea, primal, challenging, present.
Diving, literal diving, diving back to; an astounding engagement with water dived into.
Green: as an amazing engagement: green blood, green air, green out of the white of winter.
Hills, despite the prairies, granite and the antagonist. the Laurentian Shield.
A hatred of cruelty, of cruelty to cruelty.
Women make men.
The eye: symbol and *active* agent.
Concern with fish symbolic; not religion.
War is not a natural condition.
A laughter toward tourists.
Little longing for diviner regions.
(Only one Mountie – in a satire; one snowshoe.)

There are the main objective correlatives and attitudes. They add up into the word, north.

This method of thought, pattern of feeling, distinguishes the verbal texture of the modern Canadian poem. The 'phrasing', the 'fingering' – which determines the phrasing, as the pianist knows – is different; the Canadian 'phrasing' is not the American, it is certainly not the English. F. R. Scott's 'Old Song' gives the Canadian 'fingering' plain:

a quiet calling
of no mind
out of long aeons
when dust was blind
and ice hid sound

only a moving
with no note
granite lips
a stone throat

So do W. W. E. Ross's 'The Walk' and 'The Fish'. So does A. J. M. Smith's 'The Lonely Land':

This is a beauty
of dissonance,
this resonance
of stony strand,

this smoky cry
curled over a black pine
like a broken
and wind-battered branch
when the wind
bends the tips of the pines
and curdles the sky
from the north.

This is the beauty
of strength
broken by strength
and still strong.

This is not the 'fingering' of Jeffers:

This gray rock, standing tall
On the headland, where the seawind
Lets no tree grow,

Earthquake-proved, and signatured
By ages of storms; on its peak
A falcon has perched . . .

Married to the massive

Mysticism of stone,
Which failure cannot cast down
Nor success make proud.

'Mysticism' is out of texture, out of 'pace'. Smith's final stanza is not the 'pace' of Frost of New Hampshire. This difference in 'musculature' – to shift the terms from music – is found everywhere in Pratt; is unmistakable in Earle Birney's 'Bushed'.

There is the difference in 'intimacy' with nature. There are no Aphrodites in Canadian poetry – the seafoam is too cold. The Furies have to be imported. The Laurentian Shield is the intruder. There are no places for yearlong thought in a green shade.

And yet the marvels we have seen remain.
We think of the eagles, of the fawns at the river bend,
The storms, the sudden sun, the clouds sheered downwards.
('Canoe-trip': Le Pan)

INTRODUCTION

We are hitched to the seasons – four sharp ones with no south to melt into. After ice-lockings, we dive into spring. Conditions are good for spare lyricism, metaphysical wit; for an essential stability; for the green from the white.

> Fled to the green suburbs, Death
> Lies scared to death under a heap of bones.
> Beauty buds from mire
> And I, a singer in season, observe
> Death is a name for beauty not in use.
>
> ('Composition in Late Spring': Layton)

This book presents itself as a survey, from the first to the latest, of English-Canadian poetry. This does not mean all excellent poetry is represented, nor that the poet included has not written other poems of equal quality. I should like to have given more space to the poets (or some of them); but there are mechanical limits. I regret cutting lines out of dramas and narratives. I have used the earlier draft of Mair's 'Winter' – a poet getting pious is a terrible thing. The book differs from my previous Penguin Anthology, the earlier poets more solidly represented, the periods better balanced. I have still, however, emphasized contemporary poetry. It is where we live.

RALPH GUSTAFSON

New York, 1957

Foreword to the Revised Edition

THIS revised edition, coinciding with Canada's own Centennial, presents a survey of the work done in English by Canadian poets during the past one hundred years. Twenty-five years ago when the *Pelican Anthology of Canadian Poetry* introduced and published abroad the work of English-Canadian poets, the survey was made with comparative ease. There was then nothing like the present national vitality in manuscripts, readings, subsidies, prizes, broadsheets, pamphlets, private presses, periodicals, and books of poetry from the commercial houses. Centres of activity were few and localized. Isolation was the problem: pretty much as it was in Lampman's day. The general cultural climate of Canada was one of provincialism, complacency, or indifference. During the decade following World War II, those negative forces were well in retreat. The first edition of this book in 1958 was able to take advantage of a true perspective of the past, a present of rich provision, and assume a confidence in the future which one or two critics, deploying themselves from abroad, felt bound to temper. The confidence has been proved anything but misplaced. The last ten years have produced a poetry that makes historical all questioning of Canada's poetic calibre.

Editors in England and the United States of those comprehensive anthologies of 'English' poetry still ignore the work of Canadian poets. Readers should not be misled or let themselves be unconcerned. The compulsion of a figure in Canada comparable to T. S. Eliot or Ezra Pound is lacking. But the Canadian occupation is distinguished and distinguishable. I have further thoughts on what is 'Canadian'; but the premises already set forth need not be altered. The distinctive quality which I defined (not without comedy) is 'northness' (the music of Sibelius has 'northness'). And I oppose the boredom of those critics who are convinced that it does not matter who we are.

Despair is universal over the question of who everyone is. It is necessary to know. We have got ourselves into a position where perhaps this is possible. Disillusion is irreducible; the inherited past is totally questioned. Now something is happening. So radically have protests been lodged that the negations are proving no longer sufficient. We are in the midst, or at the beginning of the re-creation. The dialogue of the new Canadian poets is of the greatest interest. The burden is testamentary. It is Jonah getting himself out of the whale, caught between allegiance to a secure cynicism and declarations of his own future. The universe is cold and indifferent. The poets declare an exaltation in objectivism to the world. The heavens are mechanized. But the machinery is wonderful. Dogs treat their own kind better than man his. Love is the answer. It looks as if God is dead. He isn't. It is only that man has not made Him work. No one ran up and shook Christ's hand, Mr Kearns tells us, since he had his hand nailed down, too. The poet goes on to tell us that now he gets Christ's message: how this 'love-junk' can really hang you up for good. Black humour. Not at the expense of God. Mr Tom Marshall's 'Astrology' too leads us in an interesting direction. The philosophies are 'de-commissioned at last'. Not life.

Give me
conjunctions of dust; make again
the knotted turning of the seasons start;
give me the whole fire of your heart.

'To be mad for an answer', Mr Newlove defines the position.

Intense the de-commissioning of philosophies the world has run on, is. As intense is the determination not to be negated. These poets assert the positive Self and they ask no quarter. What they demand, as Miss MacEwen writes, is

sweet wounds which burn like stars,
stigmata of the self's own holiness,

and which

appear and plot new zodiacs upon the flesh.

By those who want disillusioned affirmation, these fresh sensibilities are not to be ignored.

Technically, the swing is from the Yeats/Eliot axis to the Pound/Williams axis. Yeats had the leisure to prophesy and warn of the Second Coming with traditional formality. These poets have not. They are in the midst of the advent of the Pitiless Beast. Immediacy and objectism are the demands; freedom from the traditional prosodic formalities. Hence, Ezra Pound and his renovations: the shift in poetic processes from 'formal' to 'open' composition. The correct objective is the achievement of greater and swifter immediacy in presenting experience; of minimal interference with the instant of cognition. The appeal is to music, to take back its own from the greatest of the arts. 'Reprendre à la musique leur bien', said Valéry of the Symbolists; 'to compose in sequence of the musical phrase, not in sequence of a metronome', as Ezra Pound put it; to overcome the displacement of tempos by metres; to overcome statics. It is to strive toward the condition of music. We return to the aesthetic of Pater, at least in this respect.

Poetry, however, is not music. Two mistakes are made. First, the error of thinking that notation is music; secondly, the error of thinking that language can communicate as music communicates. It can't. Poetry uses language. However much we strain to prevent it, poetry to be itself carries a burden of logical meaning. Music uses aural structures and is thereby dramatic. This language cannot do. Without its integument of syntax and grammatical structure, the poem is undramatic. Without the drama of syntax there is no tension. Poetry must resolve more than sound and rhythm; it must also resolve its linguistic meaning. I do not find this sad. I find this inevitable. The poet has the greater challenge.

This misadventure with music has led to the broken line, the jettisoning of metre, the placement of spaces and rests and pauses on the printed page which have so bemused and bewildered the conventional reader. The advantages gained have been several: natural breathing, 'the pressures of the breath', the physiology of cadence, modulations and juxtapositions. The method of counter-point, the fugue, the canon. Some of the modern poetic structures are as strict as serial music. Mostly, these 'liberated' poems are unholy messes – the result of not perceiving the difference between music and language, the typewriter and rhythm, the lungs and the intellect: D. H. Lawrence's 'swoonings' and Eliot's *Quartets* (I am not being religious).

Poetry is at one with music in structuring beautiful sound,

and this sound is also the meaning. The errors are in mistaking notation for music and in mistaking the conditions of music for those of language. On these two errors hang all the flaws of the prophets.

Lest it be thought that these positions are conservative and, because of an instance above, anti-Lawrence, I quote him:

> Artistic form is a revelation of the two principles of Love and the Law in a state of conflict and yet reconciled. . . . And since the two must always meet under fresh conditions, form must always be different. . . . The young artist studies maybe the method of the old great artist: but he studies chiefly to understand how the old great artist suffered in himself the conflict of Love and Law, and brought them to reconciliation . . . so that he, the young artist, may understand his own soul and gain a reconciliation between the aspiration and the resistant.

My criteria in judging such adventure (vitality) consist of three negatives. I consider dead (though it may look alive typographically) the poem (1) in which the liberation (disenfranchising of syntax, referants, metre, punctuation, or whatever convention) defeats communication, or so delays it that the poem is injured, or so assumes an arrogance that the reader is left to write the poem: when the theoretical poetry is so inaccessible that Frost's 'immortal wound' has to be self-inflicted; (2) in which the structure or the lack of structure of the line goes against natural phrasing, the instinctive physiological *and* (*nota bene*) intellectual pacing; (3) in which the manipulation is not accumulation and is not worth the poetry gained.

It is toil, this poetry. And, says Pound: 'Mais d'abord il faut être un poète'.

RALPH GUSTAFSON

Bishop's University, 1966

OLIVER GOLDSMITH

1794–1861

From *The Rising Village*

What noble courage must their hearts have fired,
How great the ardour which their souls inspired,
Who, leaving far behind their native plain,
Have sought a home beyond the western main;
And braved the terrors of the stormy seas,
In search of wealth, of freedom, and of ease!
Oh! none can tell but they who sadly share
The bosom's anguish, and its wild despair,
What dire distress awaits the hardy bands
That venture first on bleak and desert lands;
How great the pain, the danger, and the toil
Which mark the first rude culture of the soil.
When, looking round, the lonely settler sees
His home amid a wilderness of trees:
How sinks his heart in those deep solitudes,
When not a voice upon his ear intrudes;
Where solemn silence all the waste pervades,
Heightening the horror of its gloomy shades . . .

While now the Rising Village claims a name,
Its limits still increase and still its fame,
The wand'ring pedlar, who undaunted traced
His lonely footsteps o'er the silent waste;
Who traversed once the cold and snow-clad plain,
Reckless of danger, trouble or of pain,
To find a market for his little wares,
The source of all his hopes and all his cares,
Establish'd here, his settled home maintains,
And soon a merchant's higher title gains.

Around his store, on spacious shelves array'd,
Behold his great and various stock in trade!
Here nails and blankets, side by side, are seen,

There, horses' collars and a large tureen;
Buttons and tumblers, codhooks, spoons and knives,
Shawls for young damsels, flannels for old wives;
Woolcards and stockings, hats for men and boys,
Mill-saws and fenders, silks, and infants' toys;
All useful things and joined with many more,
Compose the well assorted country store . . .

The half-bred Doctor next here settles down,
And hopes the village soon will prove a town.
No rival here disputes his doubtful skill,
He cures, by chance, or ends each human ill:
By turns he physics, or his patient bleeds,
Uncertain in what case each best succeeds.
And if, from friends untimely snatch'd away,
Some beauty fall a victim to decay;
If some fine youth, his parents' fond delight,
Be early hurried to the shades of night;
Death bears the blame, 'tis his envenom'd dart
That strikes the suff'ring mortal to the heart . . .

CHARLES HEAVYSEGE

1816–76

From *Saul*

(Malzah, *the Evil Spirit from the Lord*)

Ah, weary! I am called the laughing devil.
Yet I walk up and down existence weeping . . .
How like is man unto the fallen angels!
How many in my mood now walk this world!
Some sullen at their fellows, some at fate –
From which there is no more escaping than
There is from our free wills; and some are sad
With envy at another's good, and some
With unfulfilled ambition; some with hate
Are sad, and some with love unlucky; some
With fear of missing heaven, some with dread
Of falling into hell; and many more
With curious worldly cares:– and here come Saul
And Jonathan, and both of them dejected.
We were a mournful trio, should I join them:
Grave as three owls, as sober as three storks,
More gloomy than a trinity of ravens.
In spirit, truly pitiful they show;
Portentous in appearance as yon heavens;
Or as two doctors, weighing if their patient
Shall die or live. I will approach, and listen . . .

(*The Hebrew Camp*. Saul muses.)

O life, how delicate a thing thou art,
Crushed with the feathery edge of a thin blade!
Frail! – why wert thou not made inviolable?
Why art thou irrecoverable as frail?
Thou, noblest guest, art all as much exposed
To foul ejectment from the flesh as is
The spider from its web by maiden's broom.

Yea, with a little wielded iron, any
Can drive thee forth from thy recesses' walls,
Which thou wilt not repair; for thou, weak fool,
At voice of death, from thine old banquet-room
Start'st like a haughty noble that, in huff,
Leaves his convives, and will return no more.
Why should I cherish thee, why feed thee now!
Yet I, a breathing corse, must mumble – I,
A shadow, raise my sunken, phantom maw
With the refection of this solid world . . .
All have gone from me now except despair;
And my last, lingering relics of affection –

(*After weeping awhile in silence*)

Now let me scorn all further tenderness;
And keep my heart as obdurate as the hills,
That have endured the assault of every tempest
Poured on them from the founding of the world.

(*A trumpet sounds*)

Now let me die, for I indeed was slain
With my three sons.

From *Count Filippo*

(*Of Hylas who has fallen head over heels in love with Volina*)

GALLANTIO: Now let the drums roll muffled; let the bells'
Shrill tongues toll mournfully for Hylas slain!
But though all nature should put mourning on,
Though drums be garnished with funereal crape,
My brows shall wear no less their native rose;
Though rusty drops should from the bells descend,
Dappling the upturned throats of thirsty ringers,
Adown mine own no less red wine shall flow!
We'll pledge the genius of ill luck – why not?
And draw bright laughter out of dull defeat.
PAPHIANA: Thou hast a nobler spirit than the prince. –
But is it true he plays the moribond?

GALLANTIO: Dead, dead! shot, shot to death, Paph, shot.
Yes, fairly shot, all foully shot, hath been
This representative of thirty dukes;
Each a contemner both of dart and gun.
Dead, dead is Hylas; shot, young Hylas, shot;
Banished into the air, Paph; blown point-blank
Into the world-wide welkin, shattered, shivered.
All shattered, shivered, shot; oh, shooting shame!
Shot with the bombshell of Volina's eyelid.
PAPHIANA: See here the power of woman when she wills.
GALLANTIO: True, you are powerful, and can sting like nettles,
When you are plucked by over-fearful fingers.
Volina hath her would-be stinger stung;
Teased him, as a tormenting wasp or bee
Might, in the flowery meadow, tease the steer;
Bled him to death, as butcher might a calf, –
Full many a calf hath less deserved the butcher,
Full many a butcher better quitted Cupid;
Who's shot my blue-eyed booby out of ambush;
Couching, like painted Indian 'midst the reeds,
In covert of Volina's dark eyelashes.
Now let him puff with pride of sovereign blood.
Oh, sovereign blood! oh, blood of thirty sovereigns!
Who now would give a penny for a pint
Of sovereign blood? Paph, not a pint of blood
Is in his carcass left, with love-shot riddled.
PAPHIANA: The hunter's self hath e'en been hunted down, –
The deer he stalked hath given him a gore.
GALLANTIO: Most grievously hath gored him; – but I've lost
Now faith in elegants; believe what's told
Of stalwart Samson by Delilah bound;
Of Hercules to spinning set with maids;
Of Jacob, too, who twice seven years to Laban
Did bind himself apprentice for his wives.
These bonds are good, since Hylas hath endorsed them.
PAPHIANA: These all are holy writ. But something, perhaps,
Has been forgotten in the prince's mould;
As in his ducking was Achilles' heel.

GALLANTIO: He's no Achilles, though she is a Helen, –
No Caesar he, though she as Cleopatra;
Volina lonely lingering in her bower,
Rose-pillowed, match for Egypt's magic queen. –
But as Marc Antony did lose the world
To win grand Cleopatra, so hath Hylas
Now lost his heart but hath not won Volina.

Song from *Count Filippo*

Who is lord of lordly fate, –
Lady of her lot's estate?
He who rules himself is he,
She who tempts not fate is she.

Who in peril stands of pain?
Who is sure to suffer stain?
He who climbs a thorny tree,
Gathers juicy berries she.

'*The stars are glittering in the frosty sky*'

The stars are glittering in the frosty sky,
Frequent as pebbles on a broad sea-coast;
And o'er the vault the cloud-like galaxy
Has marshalled its innumerable host.
Alive all heaven seems! with wondrous glow
Tenfold refulgent every star appears,
As if some wide, celestial gale did blow,
And thrice illume the ever-kindled spheres.
Orbs, with glad orbs rejoicing, burning, beam,
Ray-crowned, with lambent lustre in their zones,
Till o'er the blue, bespangled spaces seem
Angels and great archangels on their thrones;
A host divine, whose eyes are sparkling gems,
And forms more bright than diamond diadems.

ALEXANDER McLACHLAN

1818–96

'O! come to the greenwood shade'

O! come to the greenwood shade,
   Away from the city's din,
From the heartless strife of trade,
   And the fumes of beer and gin;
Where commerce spreads her fleets,
   Where bloated luxury lies,
And Want as she prowls the streets,
   Looks on with her wolfish eyes.

From the city with its sin,
   And its many coloured code,
Its palaces raised to gin,
   And its temples reared to God;
Its cellars dark and dank,
   Where never a sunbeam falls,
Amid faces lean and lank,
   As the hungry-looking walls.

Its festering pits of woe,
   Its teeming earthly hells,
Whose surges ever flow,
   In sound of the Sabbath bells!
O God! I would rather be
   An Indian in the wood,
And range through the forest free,
   In search of my daily food.

O! rather would I pursue,
   The wolf and the grizzly bear,
Than toil for the thankless few,
   In those seething pits of care:

Here winter's breath is rude,
And his fingers cold and wan;
But what is his wildest mood,
To the tyranny of man?

To the trackless forest wild,
To the loneliest abode;
O! the heart is reconciled,
That has felt oppression's load!
The desert place is bright,
The wilderness is fair,
If hope but shed her light, –
If freedom be but there.

CHARLES SANGSTER

1822–93

From *The St Lawrence and the Saguenay*

On, through the lovely Archipelago,
Glides the swift bark. Soft summer matins ring
From every isle. The wild fowl come and go,
Regardless of our presence. On the wing,
And perched upon the boughs, the gay birds sing
Their loves: This is their summer paradise;
From morn till night their joyous caroling
Delights the ear, and through the lucent skies
Ascends the choral hymn in softest symphonies.

The Spring is gone – light, genial-hearted Spring!
Whose breath gives odor to the violet,
Crimsons the wild rose, tints the blackbird's wing,
Unfolds the buttercup. Spring that has set
To music the laughter of the rivulet,
Sent warm pulsations through the hearts of hills,
Reclothed the forests, made the valleys wet
With pearly dew, and waked the grave old mills
From their calm sleep, by the loud rippling of the rills.

Long years ago the early Voyageurs
Gladdened these wilds with some romantic air;
The moonlight, dancing on their dripping oars,
Showed the slow batteaux passing by with care,
Impelled by rustic crews, as debonnair
As ever struck pale Sorrow dumb with Song:
Many a drooping spirit longed to share
Their pleasant melodies, that swept among
The echo-haunted woods, in accents clear and strong . . .

And now 'tis Night. A myriad stars have come
To cheer the earth, and sentinel the skies,

The full-orbed moon irradiates the gloom,
And fills the air with light. Each Islet lies
Immersed in shadow, soft as thy dark eyes;
Swift through the sinuous path our vessel glides,
Now hidden by the massive promontories,
Anon the bubbling silver from its sides
Spurning, like a wild bird, whose home is on the tides . . .

The distant knolls are soft as midnight clouds
Filled with bright memories of departed day.
Like purple glories rolling up the woods,
This rugged wilderness which we survey
Extends in wild, magnificent array,
To regions rarely trod by mortal feet.
Ev'n here, love, though we would, we cannot stay;
We cannot loiter near this calm retreat;
The Morn approaches, and his fiery steeds are fleet.

From *Sonnets*

Written in the Orillia Woods, August 1859

Blest Spirit of Calm that dwellest in these woods!
Thou art a part of that serene repose
That ofttimes lingers in the solitudes
Of my lone heart, when the tumultuous throes
Of some vast Grief have borne me to the earth.
For I have fought with Sorrow face to face;
Have tasted of the cup that brings to some
A frantic madness and delirious mirth,
But prayed and trusted for the light to come,
To break the gloom and darkness of the place.
Through the dim aisles the sunlight penetrates,
And nature's self rejoices; heaven's light
Comes down into my heart, and in its might
My soul stands up and knocks at God's own temple-gates.

CHARLES MAIR

1838–1927

Winter

When gadding snow makes hill-sides white,
  And icicles form more and more;
When niggard Frost stands all the night,
  And taps at snoring Gaffer's door;
When watch-dogs bay the vagrant wind,
  And shiv'ring kine herd close in shed;
When kitchens chill, and maids unkind,
  Send rustic suitors home to bed –
    Then do I say the winter cold,
    It seems to me, is much too bold.

When winking sparks run up the stalk,
  And faggots blaze within the grate,
And, by the ingle-cheek, I talk
  With shadows from the realm of fate;
When authors old, yet ever young,
  Look down upon me from the walls,
And songs by spirit-lips are sung
  To pleasant tunes and madrigals, –
    Then do I say the winter cold
    Brings back to me the joys of old.

When morn is bleak, and sunshine cool,
  And trav'llers' beards with rime are grey;
When frost-nipt urchins weep in school,
  And sleighs creak o'er the drifted way;
When smoke goes quick from chimney-top,
  And mist flies through the open hatch;
When snow-flecks to the window hop,
  And children's tongues cling to the latch, –
    Then do I sigh for summer wind,
    And wish the winter less unkind.

When merry bells a-jingling go,
  And prancing horses beat the ground;
When youthful hearts are all aglow,
  And youthful gladness rings around;
When gallants praise, and maidens blush
  To hear their charms so loudly told,
Whilst echoing vale and echoing bush
  Halloo their laughter, fold on fold, –
    Then do I think the winter meet,
    For gallants free and maidens sweet.

When great pines crack with mighty sound,
  And ice doth rift with doleful moan;
When luckless wanderers are found
  Quite stiff in wooded valleys lone;
When ragged mothers have no sheet
  To shield their babes from winter's flaw;
When milk is frozen in the teat,
  And beggars shiver in their straw, –
    Then do I hate the winter's cheer,
    And weep for springtime of the year.

When ancient hosts their guests do meet,
  And fetch old jorums from the bin;
When viols loud and dancers' feet
  In lofty halls make mickle din;
When jokes pass round, and nappy ale
  Sends pleasure mounting to the brain;
When hours are filched from night so pale,
  And youngsters sigh and maids are fain, –
    Then do I hail the wintry breeze
  Which brings such ripened joys as these.

But, when the winter chills my friend,
  And steals the heart-fire from his breast;
Or woos the ruffian wind to send
  One pang to rob him of his rest–
All gainless grows the Christmas cheer,

And gloomy seems the new year's light,
For joy but lives when friends are near,
And dies when they do quit the sight. –
Then, winter, do I cry, 'thy greed
Is great, ay, thou art cold indeed!'

From *Tecumseh*

(*A grove in front of General Harrison's House, Vincennes, Indiana Territory*)

TECUMSEH: Once we were strong.
Once all this mighty continent was ours,
And the Great Spirit made it for our use.
He knew no boundaries, so had we peace
In the vast shelter of His handiwork,
And, happy here, we cared not whence we came.
We brought no evils thence – no treasured hate,
No greed of gold, no quarrels over God;
And so our broils, to narrow issues joined,
Were soon composed, and touched the ground of peace.
Our very ailments, rising from the earth,
And not from any foul abuse in us,
Drew back, and let age ripen to death's hand.
Thus flowed our lives until your people came,
Till from the East our matchless misery came!
Since then our tale is crowded with your crimes,
With broken faith, with plunder of reserves –
The sacred remnants of our wide domain –
With tamp'rings, and delirious feasts of fire,
The fruit of your thrice-cursed stills of death,
Which make our good men bad, our bad men worse,
Aye! blind them till they grope in open day,
And stumble into miserable graves.
Oh, it is piteous, for none will hear!
There is no hand to help, no heart to feel,
No tongue to plead for us in all your land.
But every hand aims death, and every heart,

Ulcered with hate, resents our presence here;
And every tongue cries for our children's land
To expiate their crime of being born.
Oh, we have ever yielded in the past,
But we shall yield no more! Those plains are ours!
Those forests are our birth-right and our home!
Let not the Long-Knife build one cabin there –
Or fire from it will spread to every roof,
To compass you, and light your souls to death!

(Act II, sc. iv)

Long-Knife: the American.

GEORGE T. LANIGAN

1846–86

A Threnody

'The Ahkoond of Swat is dead.' – Press Dispatch

What, what, what,
What's the news from Swat?
        Sad news,
        Bad news,
Comes by the cable led
Through the Indian Ocean's bed,
Through the Persian Gulf, the Red
Sea and the Med-
Iterranean – he's dead;
The Ahkoond is dead!

For the Ahkoond I mourn.
        Who wouldn't?
He strove to disregard the message stern,
        But he Ahkoondn't.

Dead, dead, dead;
        Sorrow, Swats!
Swats wha' hae wi' Ahkoond bled,
Swats whom he had often led
Onward to a gory bed,
Or to victory,
        As the case might be.
        Sorrow, Swats!
Tears shed,
        Shed tears like water,
Your great Ahkoond is dead!
        That Swat's the matter!

Mourn, city of Swat!
Your great Ahkoond is not,

But lain 'mid worms to rot:
His mortal part alone, his soul was caught
(Because he was a good Ahkoond)
Up to the bosom of Mahound.
Though earthly walls his frame surround
(For ever hallowed be the ground!)
And sceptics mock the lowly mound
And say, 'He's now of no Ahkound!'
(His soul is in the skies!)
The azure skies that bend above his loved
    Metropolis of Swat
He sees with larger, other eyes,
Athwart all earthly mysteries –
    He knows what's Swat.

Let Swat bury the great Ahkoond
    With a noise of mourning and of lamentation!
Let Swat bury the great Ahkoond
    With the noise of the mourning of the Swattish nation!
        Fallen is at length
        Its tower of strength,
Its sun had dimmed ere it had nooned:
Dead lies the great Ahkoond,
        The great Ahkoond of Swat
        Is not.

ISABELLA VALANCY CRAWFORD

1850–87

True and False

Oh! spring was in his shining eyes
 And summer in his happy soul;
He bounded o'er the misty rise
 And saw the purple ocean roll.

With stars above and stars below,
 The lovely eve was fair as noon;
He saw above him richly glow
 The white shores of the sailing moon,

Her vales of jet, her pearly peaks,
 The lustre on her shining sands;
Leaped eager roses to his cheeks –
 He cried, 'I seek her silver strands!'

There rose a siren where the foam
 Of ocean sparkled most with stars:
She combed gold locks with golden comb;
 She floated past the murmuring bars.

She sang so loud, so silvery clear,
 The trees in far woods seemed to stir,
And seaward lean; from lake and mere
 Rushed eager rivers down to her.

She swept in mist of far blown hair,
 Star-white, from glittering steep to steep;
She loved his gay and dauntless air –
 Rose loftier from the purple deep,

Till, whiter than white coral rocks,
 She glimmered high against the moon.

And oh, she loved his raven locks!
  And oh, she sang him to his doom!

'O boy, why dost thou upward turn
  The crystal of thy youthful eyes?
The true moon in the sea doth burn;
  Far 'neath my silver feet she lies.

'Look down, look down, and thou shalt see
  A fairer moon and mellower stars;
A shadow pale and wan is she
  That floats o'er heaven's azure bars.

'Look down, look down – the true moon lies
  Deep in mid-ocean's fairest part;
Nor let that wan shade on the skies
  Draw all the tides of thy young heart.

'O let mine arms thy neck entwine!
  O boy, come down to me, to me!
I'll bring thee where the moon doth shine,
  The round moon in the silver sea.'

He heard the song, he felt the spell,
  He saw her white hand beckon on,
Believed the tale she sang so well,
  Beheld the moon that falsely shone.

The true moon wheeled her silver isle
  Serene in heaven's blue mystery;
He sank in those white arms of guile
  To seek the false moon in the sea.

The Song of the Arrow

(From *Gisli, the Chieftain*)

What know I,
As I bite the blue veins of the throbbing sky,
To the quarry's breast,
Hot from the sides of the sleek, smooth nest?

What know I
Of the will of the tense bow from which I fly?
What the need or jest
That feathers my flight to its bloody rest?

What know I
Of the will of the bow that speeds me on high?
What doth the shrill bow
Of the hand on its singing soul-string know?

Flame-swift speed I,
And the dove and the eagle shriek out and die.
Whence comes my sharp zest
For the heart of the quarry? The gods know best.

The Dark Stag

A startled stag, the blue-grey Night,
Leaps down beyond black pines.
Behind – a length of yellow light –
The hunter's arrow shines:
His moccasins are stained with red,
He bends upon his knee,
From covering peaks his shafts are sped,
The blue mists plume his mighty head –
Well may the swift Night flee!

The pale, pale Moon, a snow-white doe,
Bounds by his dappled flank:

They beat the stars down as they go,
  Like wood-bells growing rank.
The winds lift dewlaps from the ground,
  Leap from the quaking reeds;
Their hoarse bays shake the forest round,
With keen cries on the track they bound –
  Swift, swift the dark stag speeds!

Away! his white doe, far behind,
  Lies wounded on the plain;
Yells at his flank the nimblest wind,
  His large tears fall in rain;
Like lily pads, small clouds grow white
  About his darkling way;
From his bald nest upon the height
The red-eyed eagle sees his flight;
He falters, turns, the antlered Night –
  The dark stag stands at bay!

His feet are in the waves of space;
  His antlers broad and dun
He lowers; he turns his velvet face
  To front the hunter, Sun;
He stamps the lilied clouds, and high
  His branches fill the west.
The lean stork sails across the sky,
The shy loon shrieks to see him die,
  The winds leap at his breast.

Roar the rent lakes as thro' the wave
  Their silver warriors plunge,
As vaults from core of crystal cave
  The strong, fierce muskallunge;
Red torches of the sumach glare,
  Fall's council-fires are lit;
The bittern, squaw-like, scolds the air;
The wild duck splashes loudly where
  The rustling rice-spears knit.

Shaft after shaft the red Sun speeds:
  Rent the stag's dappled side,
His breast, fanged by the shrill winds, bleeds,
  He staggers on the tide;
He feels the hungry waves of space
  Rush at him high and blue;
Their white spray smites his dusky face,
Swifter the Sun's fierce arrows race
  And pierce his stout heart thro'.

His antlers fall; once more he spurns
  The hoarse hounds of the day;
His blood upon the crisp blue burns,
  Reddens the mounting spray;
His branches smite the wave – with cries
  The loud winds pause and flag –
He sinks in space – red glow the skies,
The brown earth crimsons as he dies,
  The strong and dusky stag.

The Lily Bed

His cedar paddle, scented, red,
He thrust down through the lily bed;

Cloaked in a golden pause he lay,
Locked in the arms of the placid bay.

Trembled alone his bark canoe
As shocks of bursting lilies flew

Thro' the still crystal of the tide,
And smote the frail boat's birchen side;

Or, when beside the sedges thin
Rose the sharp silver of a fin;

Or when, a wizard swift and cold,
A dragon-fly beat out in gold

And jewels all the widening rings
Of waters singing to his wings;

Or, like a winged and burning soul,
Dropped from the gloom an oriole

On the cool wave, as to the balm
Of the Great Spirit's open palm

The freed soul flies. And silence clung
To the still hours, as tendrils hung,

In darkness carven, from the trees,
Sedge-buried to their burly knees.

Stillness sat in his lodge of leaves;
Clung golden shadows to its eaves,

And on its cone-spiced floor, like maize,
Red-ripe, fell sheaves of knotted rays.

The wood, a proud and crested brave;
Bead-bright, a maiden, stood the wave.

And he had spoke his soul of love
With voice of eagle and of dove.

Of loud, strong pines his tongue was made;
His lips, soft blossoms in the shade,

That kissed her silver lips – her's cool
As lilies on his inmost pool –

Till now he stood, in triumph's rest,
His image painted in her breast.

One isle 'tween blue and blue did melt, –
A bead of wampum from the belt

Of Manitou – a purple rise
On the far shore heaved to the skies.

His cedar paddle, scented, red,
He drew up from the lily bed;

All lily-locked, all lily-locked,
His light bark in the blossoms rocked.

Their cool lips round the sharp prow sang,
Their soft clasp to the frail sides sprang,

With breast and lip they wove a bar.
Stole from her lodge the Evening Star;

With golden hand she grasped the mane
Of a red cloud on her azure plain.

It by the peaked, red sunset flew;
Cool winds from its bright nostrils blew.

They swayed the high, dark trees, and low
Swept the locked lilies to and fro.

With cedar paddle, scented, red,
He pushed out from the lily bed.

GEORGE FREDERICK CAMERON

1854–85

My Political Faith

I am not of those fierce, wild wills,
  Albeit from loins of warlike line,
  To wreck laws human and divine
Alike, that on a million ills
  I might erect one sacred shrine

To Freedom: nor again am I
  Of *these* who could be sold and bought
  To fall before a Juggernaut:
I hold all 'royal right' a lie —
  Save that a royal soul hath wrought!

It is in the extreme begins
  And ends all danger: if the Few
  Would feel, or if the Many knew
This fact, the mass of fewer sins
  Would shrive them in their passing through:

O'er all God's footstool not a slave
  Should under his great glory stand,
  For men would rise, swift sword in hand,
And give each tyrant to his grave
  And freedom to each lovely land.

Relics

Put them aside – I hate the sight of them! –
  That golden wonder from her golden hair –
  That faded lily which she once did wear
Upon her bosom – and that cold hard gem
  Which glittered on her taper finger fair.

They are of her, and, being so, they must
  Bé like to her, and she is all a lie
  That seems a truth when truth is not a-nigh, –
A thing whose love is light as balance dust,
  I loved her once, I love – nay, put them by!

Conceal them like the dead from sight away!
  I must forget her and she was so dear
  In former times! I could not bear them near:
Let them be sealed forever from the day –
  Be wrapt in darkness, shrouded – buried here

Where never more my eye may rest on them!
  This golden wonder from her golden hair –
  This faded lily that she once did wear
Upon her bosom – and this joyless gem
  That glittered on her taper finger fair.

Standing on Tiptoe

Standing on tiptoe ever since my youth
  Striving to grasp the future just above,
I hold at length the only future – Truth,
  And Truth is Love.

I feel as one who being awhile confined
  Sees drop to dust about him all his bars:–
The clay grows less, and, leaving it, the mind
  Dwells with the stars.

WILLIAM HENRY DRUMMOND

1854–1907

The Wreck of the 'Julie Plante'

A Legend of Lac St Pierre

On wan dark night on Lac St Pierre,
  De win' she blow, blow, blow,
An' de crew of de wood scow 'Julie Plante'
  Got scar't an' run below –
For de win' she blow lak hurricane
  Bimeby she blow some more,
An' de scow bus' up on Lac St Pierre
  Wan arpent from de shore.

De captinne walk on de fronte deck,
  An' walk de hin' deck too –
He call de crew from up de hole
  He call de cook also.
De cook she's name was Rosie,
  She come from Montreal,
Was chambre maid on lumber barge,
  On de Grande Lachine Canal.

De win' she blow from nor'-eas'-wes', –
  De sout' win' she blow too,
W'en Rosie cry 'Mon cher captinne,
  Mon cher, w'at I shall do?'
Den de Captinne t'row de big ankerre,
  But still de scow she dreef,
De crew he can't pass on de shore,
  Becos' he los' hees skeef.

De night was dark lak' wan black cat,
  De wave run high an' fas',
W'en de captinne tak' de Rosie girl
  An' tie her to de mas'.

Den he also tak' de life preserve,
  An' jomp off on de lak',
An' say, 'Good-bye, ma Rosie dear,
  I go drown for your sak'.'

Nex' morning very early
  'Bout ha'f-pas' two – t'ree – four –
De captinne – scow – an' de poor Rosie
  Was corpses on de shore,
For de win' she blow lak' hurricane
  Bimeby she blow some more,
An' de scow bus' up on Lac St Pierre,
  Wan arpent from de shore.

MORAL

Now all good wood scow sailor man
  Tak' warning by dat storm
An' go an' marry some nice French girl
  An' leev on wan beeg farm.
De win' can blow lak' hurricane
  An' s'pose she blow some more,
You can't get drown on Lac St Pierre
  So long you stay on shore.

WILFRED CAMPBELL

1858–1918

How One Winter Came in the Lake Region

For weeks and weeks the autumn world stood still,
  Clothed in the shadow of a smoky haze;
The fields were dead, the wind had lost its will,
And all the lands were hushed by wood and hill,
  In those grey, withered days.

Behind the blear sun rose and set,
  At night the moon would nestle in a cloud;
The fisherman, a ghost, did cast his net;
The lake its shores forgot to chafe and fret,
  And hushed its caverns loud.

Far in the smoky woods the birds were mute,
  Save that from blackened tree a jay would scream,
Or far in swamps, the lizard's lonesome lute
Would pipe in thirst, or by some gnarlèd root
  The tree-toad trilled his dream.

From day to day still hushed the season's mood,
  The streams stayed in their runnels shrunk and dry;
Suns rose aghast by wave and shore and wood,
And all the world, with ominous silence, stood
  In weird expectancy:

When one strange night the sun like blood went down,
  Flooding the heavens in a ruddy hue;
Red grew the lake, the sere fields parched and brown,
Red grew the marshes where the creeks stole down,
  But never a wind-breath blew.

That night I felt the winter in my veins,
　A joyous tremor of the icy glow;
And woke to hear the north's wild vibrant strains,
While far and wide, by withered woods and plains,
　Fast fell the driving snow.

JOHN FREDERIC HERBIN

1860–1923

Haying

From the soft dyke-road, crooked and waggon-worn,
Comes the great load of rustling scented hay,
Slow-drawn with heavy swing and creaky sway
Through the cool freshness of the windless morn.
The oxen, yoked and sturdy, horn to horn,
Sharing the rest and toil of night and day,
Bend head and neck to the long hilly way
By many a season's labour marked and torn.
On the broad sea of dyke the gathering heat
Waves upward from the grass, where road on road
Is swept before the tramping of the teams.
And while the oxen rest beside the sweet
New hay, the loft receives the early load,
With hissing stir, among the dusty beams.

CHARLES G. D. ROBERTS

1860–1943

Marsyas

A little grey hill-glade, close-turfed, withdrawn
Beyond resort or heed of trafficking feet,
Ringed round with slim trunks of the mountain ash.
Through the slim trunks and scarlet bunches flash –
Beneath the clear chill glitterings of the dawn –
Far off, the crests, where down the rosy shore
The Pontic surges beat.
The plains lie dim below. The thin airs wash
The circuit of the autumn-coloured hills,
And this high glade, whereon
The satyr pipes, who soon shall pipe no more.
He sits against the beech-tree's mighty bole, –
He leans, and with persuasive breathing fills
The happy shadows of the slant-set lawn.
The goat-feet fold beneath a gnarlèd root;
And sweet, and sweet the note that steals and thrills
From slender stops of that shy flute.
Then to the goat-feet comes the wide-eyed fawn
Hearkening; the rabbits fringe the glade, and lay
Their long ears to the sound;
In the pale boughs the partridge gather round,
And quaint hern from the sea-green river reeds;
The wild ram halts upon a rocky horn
O'erhanging; and, unmindful of his prey,
The leopard steals with narrowed lids to lay
His spotted length along the ground.
The thin airs wash, the thin clouds wander by,
And those hushed listeners move not. All the morn
He pipes, soft-swaying, and with half-shut eye,
In rapt content of utterance, –

nor heeds
The young god standing in his branchy place,

The languor on his lips, and in his face,
Divinely inaccessible, the scorn.

Canada

O Child of Nations, giant-limbed,
Who stand'st among the nations now
Unheeded, unadorned, unhymned,
With unanointed brow, –

How long the ignoble sloth, how long
The trust in greatness not thine own?
Surely the lion's brood is strong
To front the world alone!

How long the indolence, ere thou dare
Achieve thy destiny, seize thy fame, –
Ere our proud eyes behold thee bear
A nation's franchise, nation's name?

The Saxon force, the Celtic fire,
These are thy manhood's heritage!
Why rest with babes and slaves? Seek higher
The place of race and age.

I see to every wind unfurled
The flag that bears the Maple Wreath;
Thy swift keels furrow round the world
Its blood-red folds beneath;

Thy swift keels cleave the furthest seas;
Thy white sails swell with alien gales;
To stream on each remotest breeze
The black smoke of thy pipes exhales.

O Falterer, let thy past convince
Thy future, – all the growth, the gain,

The fame since Cartier knew thee, since
  Thy shores beheld Champlain!

Montcalm and Wolfe! Wolfe and Montcalm!
  Quebec, thy storied citadel
Attest in burning song and psalm
  How here thy heroes fell!

O Thou that bor'st the battle's brunt
  At Queenston and at Lundy's Lane, –
On whose scant ranks but iron front
  The battle broke in vain! –

Whose was the danger, whose the day,
  From whose triumphant throats the cheers,
At Chrysler's Farm, at Chateauguay,
  Storming like clarion-bursts our ears?

On soft Pacific slopes, – beside
  Strange floods that northward rave and fall, –
Where chafes Acadia's chainless tide –
  Thy sons await thy call.

They wait; but some in exile, some
  With strangers housed, in stranger lands, –
And some Canadian lips are dumb
  Beneath Egyptian sands.

O mystic Nile! Thy secret yields
  Before us; thy most ancient dreams
Are mixed with far Canadian fields
  And murmur of Canadian streams.

But thou, my country, dream not thou!
  Wake, and behold how night is done, –
How on thy breast, and o'er thy brow,
  Bursts the uprising sun!

CHARLES G. D. ROBERTS

Three Sonnets

From *Songs of the Common Day*

The Pea-fields

These are the fields of light, and laughing air,
  And yellow butterflies, and foraging bees,
  And whitish, wayward blossoms winged as these,
And pale green tangles like a seamaid's hair.
Pale, pale the blue, but pure beyond compare,
  And pale the sparkle of the far-off seas,
  A-shimmer like these fluttering slopes of peas,
And pale the open landscape everywhere.

From fence to fence a perfumed breath exhales
  O'er the bright pallor of the well-loved fields, –
My fields of Tantramar in summer-time;
  And, scorning the poor feed their pasture yields,
Up from the bushy lots the cattle climb,
  To gaze with longing through the grey, mossed rails.

The Herring Weir

Back to the green deeps of the outer bay
  The red and amber currents glide and cringe,
  Diminishing behind a luminous fringe
Of cream-white surf and wandering wraiths of spray.
Stealthily, in the old reluctant way,
  The red flats are uncovered, mile on mile,
  To glitter in the sun a golden while.
Far down the flats, a phantom sharply grey,
The herring weir emerges, quick with spoil.
  Slowly the tide forsakes it. Then draws near,
  Descending from the farm-house on the height,
A cart, with gaping tubs. The oxen toil
  Sombrely o'er the level to the weir,
  And drag a long black trail across the light.

CHARLES G. D. ROBERTS

The Flight of the Geese

I hear the low wind wash the softening snow,
  The low tide loiter down the shore. The night
  Full filled with April forecast, hath no light.
The salt wave on the sedge-flat pulses slow.
Through the hid furrows lisp in murmurous flow
  The thaw's shy ministers; and hark! The height
  Of heaven grows weird and loud with unseen flight
Of strong hosts prophesying as they go!

High through the drenched and hollow night their wings
  Beat northward hard on winter's trail. The sound
Of their confused and solemn voices, borne
Athwart the dark to their long Arctic morn,
  Comes with a sanction and an awe profound,
A boding of unknown, foreshadowed things.

At Tide Water

The red and yellow of the Autumn salt-grass,
  The grey flats, and the yellow-grey full tide,
The lonely stacks, the grave expanse of marshes, –
  O Land wherein my memories abide,
I have come back that you may make me tranquil,
  Resting a little at your heart of peace,
Remembering much amid your serious leisure,
  Forgetting more amid your large release.
For yours the wisdom of the night and morning,
  The word of the inevitable years,
The open heaven's unobscured communion,
  And the dim whisper of the wheeling spheres.
The great things and the terrible I bring you,
  To be illumined in your spacious breath, –
Love, and the ashes of desire, and anguish,
  Strange laughter, and the unhealing wound of death.

These in the world, all these, have come upon me,
  Leaving me mute and shaken with surprise.
Oh, turn them in your measureless contemplation,
  And in their mastery teach me to be wise.

In the Night Watches

When the little spent winds are at rest in the tamarack tree
In the still of the night,
And the moon in her waning is wan and misshapen,
And out on the lake
The loon floats in a glimmer of light,
And the solitude sleeps, –
Then I lie in my bunk wide awake,
And my long thoughts stab me with longing,
Alone in my shack by the marshes of lone Margaree.

Far, oh so far in the forests of silence they lie,
The lake and the marshes of lone Margaree,
And no man comes my way.
Of spruce logs my cabin is builded securely;
With slender spruce saplings its bark roof is battened down surely;
In its rafters the mice are at play,
With rustlings furtive and shy,
In the still of the night.

Awake, wide-eyed, I watch my window-square,
Pallid and grey.
(O Memory, pierce me not! O Longing, stab me not!
O ache of longing memory, pass me by, and spare,
And let me sleep!)
Once and again the loon cries from the lake.
Though no breath stirs
The ghostly tamaracks and the brooding firs,
Something as light as air leans on my door.

Is it an owl's wing brushes at my latch?
Are they of foxes, those light feet that creep
Outside, light as fall'n leaves
On the forest floor?
From the still lake I hear
A feeding trout rise to some small night fly.
The splash, how sharply clear!
Almost I see the wide, slow ripple circling to the shore.

The spent winds are at rest. But my heart, spent and faint, is unresting.
Long, long a stranger to peace . . .
O so Dear, O so Far, O so Unforgotten-in-dream,
Somewhere in the world, somewhere beyond reach of my questing.
Beyond seas, beyond years,
You will hear my heart in your sleep, and you will stir restlessly;
You will stir at the touch of my hand on your hair;
You will wake with a start,
With my voice in your ears
And an old, old ache at your heart,
(In the still of the night)
And your pillow wet with tears.

The Aim

O Thou who lovest not alone
The swift success, the instant goal,
But hast a lenient eye to mark
The failures of the inconstant soul,

Consider not my little worth, –
The mean achievement, scamped in act,
The high resolve and low result,
The dream that durst not face the fact.

But count the reach of my desire.
Let this be something in Thy sight: –

I have not, in the slothful dark,
Forgot the Vision and the Height.

Neither my body nor my soul
To earth's low ease will yield consent.
I praise Thee for my will to strive.
I bless Thy goad of discontent.

ARCHIBALD LAMPMAN

1861–99

Heat

From plains that reel to southward, dim,
  The road runs by me white and bare;
Up the steep hill it seems to swim
  Beyond, and melt into the glare.
Upward half way, or it may be
  Nearer the summit, slowly steals
A hay-cart, moving dustily
  With idly clacking wheels.

By his cart's side the wagoner
  Is slouching slowly at his ease,
Half-hidden in the windless blur
  Of white dust puffing to his knees.
This wagon on the height above,
From sky to sky on either hand,
Is the sole thing that seems to move
  In all the heat-held land.

Beyond me in the fields the sun
  Soaks in the grass and hath his will;
I count the marguerites one by one;
  Even the buttercups are still.
On the brook yonder not a breath
Disturbs the spider or the midge.
The water-bugs draw close beneath
  The cool gloom of the bridge.

Where the far elm-tree shadows flood
  Dark patches in the burning grass,
The cows, each with her peaceful cud,
  Lie waiting for the heat to pass.

From somewhere on the slope near by
  Into the pale depth of the noon
A wandering thrush slides leisurely
  His thin revolving tune.

In intervals of dreams I hear
  The cricket from the droughty ground;
The grass-hoppers spin into mine ear
  A small innumerable sound.
I lift mine eyes sometimes to gaze:
  The burning sky-line blinds my sight:
The woods far off are blue with haze:
  The hills are drenched in light.

And yet to me not this or that
  Is always sharp or always sweet;
In the sloped shadow of my hat
  I lean at rest, and drain the heat;
Nay more, I think some blessèd power
  Hath brought me wandering idly here:
In the full furnace of this hour
  My thoughts grow keen and clear.

Life and Nature

I passed through the gates of the city,
  The streets were strange and still,
Through the doors of the open churches
  The organs were moaning shrill.

Through the doors and the great high windows
  I heard the murmur of prayer,
And the sound of their solemn singing
  Streamed out on the sunlit air;

A sound of some great burden
  That lay on the world's dark breast,

Of the old, and the sick, and the lonely,
And the weary that cried for rest.

I strayed through the midst of the city
Like one distracted or mad.
'Oh, Life! Oh, Life!' I kept saying,
And the very word seemed sad.

I passed through the gates of the city,
And I heard the small birds sing,
I laid me down in the meadows
Afar from the bell-ringing.

In the depth and the bloom of the meadows
I lay on the earth's quiet breast,
The poplar fanned me with shadows,
And the veery sang me to rest.

Blue, blue was the heaven above me,
And the earth green at my feet;
'Oh, Life! Oh, Life!' I kept saying,
And the very word seemed sweet.

September

Now hath the summer reached her golden close,
And, lost amid her corn-fields, bright of soul,
Scarcely perceives from her divine repose
How near, how swift, the inevitable goal:
Still, still, she smiles, though from her careless feet
The bounty and the fruitful strength are gone,
And through the soft long wondering days goes on
The silent sere decadence sad and sweet.

The kingbird and the pensive thrush are fled,
Children of light, too fearful of the gloom;
The sun falls low, the secret word is said,
The mouldering woods grow silent as the tomb;

Even the fields have lost their sovereign grace,
 The cone-flower and the marguerite; and no more,
 Across the river's shadow-haunted floor,
The paths of skimming swallows interlace.

Already in the outland wilderness
 The forests echo with unwonted dins;
In clamorous gangs the gathering woodmen press
 Northward, and the stern winter's toil begins.
Around the long low shanties, whose rough lines
 Break the sealed dreams of many an unnamed lake,
 Already in the frost-clear morns awake
The crash and thunder of the falling pines.

Where the tilled earth, with all its fields set free,
 Naked and yellow from the harvest lies,
By many a loft and busy granary,
 The hum and tumult of the thrashers rise;
There the tanned farmers labor without slack,
 Till twilight deepens round the spouting mill,
 Feeding the loosened sheaves, or with fierce will,
Pitching waist-deep upon the dusty stack.

Still a brief while, ere the old year quite pass,
 Our wandering steps and wistful eyes shall greet
The leaf, the water, the belovèd grass;
 Still from these haunts and this accustomed seat
I see the wood-wrapt city, swept with light,
 The blue long-shadowed distance, and, between,
 The dotted farm-lands with their parcelled green,
The dark pine forest and the watchful height.

I see the broad rough meadow stretched away
 Into the crystal sunshine, wastes of sod,
Acres of withered vervain, purple-grey,
 Branches of aster, groves of goldenrod;
And yonder, toward the sunlit summit, strewn
 With shadowy boulders, crowned and swathed with weed,

Stand ranks of silken thistles, blown to seed,
Long silver fleeces shining like the noon.

In far-off russet corn-fields, where the dry
Gray shocks stand peaked and withering, half concealed
In the rough earth, the orange pumpkins lie,
Full-ribbed; and in the windless pasture-field
The sleek red horses o'er the sun-warmed ground
Stand pensively about in companies,
While all around them from the motionless trees
The long clean shadows sleep without a sound.

Under the cool elm-trees floats the distant stream,
Moveless as air; and o'er the vast warm earth
The fathomless daylight seems to stand and dream,
A liquid cool elixir – all its girth
Bound with faint haze, a frail transparency,
Whose lucid purple barely veils and fills
The utmost valleys and the thin last hills,
Nor mars one whit their perfect clarity.

Thus without grief the golden days go by,
So soft we scarcely notice how they wend,
And like a smile half happy, or a sigh,
The summer passes to her quiet end;
And soon, too soon, around the cumbered eaves
Sly frosts shall take the creepers by surprise,
And through the wind-touched reddening woods shall rise
October with the rain of ruined leaves.

Solitude

How still it is here in the woods. The trees
Stand motionless, as if they do not dare
To stir, lest it should break the spell. The air
Hangs quiet as spaces in a marble frieze.
Even this little brook, that runs at ease,

Whispering and gurgling in its knotted bed,
Seems but to deepen with its curling thread
Of sound the shadowy sun-pierced silences.

Sometimes a hawk screams or a woodpecker
Startles the stillness from its fixèd mood
With his loud careless tap. Sometimes I hear
The dreamy white-throat from some far-off tree
Pipe slowly on the listening solitude
His five pure notes succeeding pensively.

A Summer Evening

The clouds grow clear, the pine-wood glooms and stills
With brown reflections in the silent bay,
And far beyond the pale blue-misted hills
The rose and purple evening dreams away.
The thrush, the veery, from mysterious dales
Rings his last round; and outward like a sea
The shining, shadowy heart of heaven unveils
The starry legend of eternity.
The day's long troubles lose their sting and pass.
Peaceful the world, and peaceful grows my heart.
The gossip cricket from the friendly grass
Talks of old joys and takes the dreamer's part.
Then night, the healer, with unnoticed breath,
And sleep, dark sleep, so near, so like to death.

Winter Evening

To-night the very horses springing by
Toss gold from whitened nostrils. In a dream
The streets that narrow to the westward gleam
Like rows of golden palaces; and high
From all the crowded chimneys tower and die
A thousand aureoles. Down in the west

The brimming plains beneath the sunset rest,
One burning sea of gold. Soon, soon shall fly
The glorious vision, and the hours shall feel
A mightier master; soon from height to height,
With silence and the sharp unpitying stars,
Stern creeping frosts, and winds that touch like steel,
Out of the depth beyond the eastern bars,
Glittering and still shall come the awful night.

Among the Orchards

Already in the dew-wrapped vineyards dry
Dense weights of heat press down. The large bright drops
Shrink in the leaves. From dark acacia tops
The nut-hatch flings his short reiterate cry;
And ever as the sun mounts hot and high
Thin voices crowd the grass. In soft long strokes
The wind goes murmuring through the mountain oaks.
Faint wefts creep out along the blue and die.
I hear far in among the motionless trees –
Shadows that sleep upon the shaven sod –
The thud of dropping apples. Reach on reach
Stretch plots of perfumed orchard, where the bees
Murmur among the full-fringed goldenrod
Or cling half-drunken to the rotting peach.

Midnight

From where I sit, I see the stars,
  And down the chilly floor
The moon between the frozen bars
  Is glimmering dim and hoar.

Without in many a peakèd mound
  The glinting snowdrifts lie;
There is no voice or living sound;
  The embers slowly die.

Yet some wild thing is in mine ear;
  I hold my breath and hark;
Out of the depth I seem to hear
  A crying in the dark:

No sound of man or wife or child,
  No sound of beast that groans,
Or of the wind that whistles wild,
  Or of the tree that moans:

I know not what it is I hear;
  I bend my head and hark:
I cannot drive it from mine ear,
  That crying in the dark.

Snow

White are the far-off plains, and white
  The fading forests grow;
The wind dies out along the height,
  And denser still the snow,
A gathering weight on roof and tree,
  Falls down scarce audibly.

The road before me smooths and fills
  Apace, and all about
The fences dwindle, and the hills
  Are blotted slowly out;
The naked trees loom spectrally
  Into the dim white sky.

The meadows and far-sheeted streams
  Lie still without a sound;
Like some soft minister of dreams
  The snow-fall hoods me round;
In wood and water, earth and air,
  A silence everywhere.

Save when at lonely intervals
Some farmer's sleigh, urged on,
With rustling runners and sharp bells,
Swings by me and is gone;
Or from the empty waste I hear
A sound remote and clear;

The barking of a dog, or call
To cattle, sharply pealed,
Borne echoing from some wayside stall
Or barnyard far afield;
Then all is silent, and the snow
Falls, settling soft and slow.

The evening deepens, and the gray
Folds closer earth and sky;
The world seems shrouded far away;
Its noises sleep, and I,
As secret as yon buried stream,
Plod dumbly on, and dream.

Refuge

Where swallows and wheatfields are,
O hamlet brown and still,
O river that shineth far,
By meadow, pier, and mill:

O endless sunsteeped plain,
With forests in dim blue shrouds,
And little wisps of rain,
Falling from far-off clouds:

I come from the choking air
Of passion, doubt, and strife,
With a spirit and mind laid bare
To your healing breadth of life:

O fruitful and sacred ground,
 O sunlight and summer sky,
Absorb me and fold me round,
 For broken and tired am I.

Winter-Solitude

I saw the city's towers on a luminous pale-gray sky;
Beyond them a hill of the softest mistiest green,
With naught but frost and the coming night between,
And a long thin cloud above it the colour of August rye.

I saw in the midst of a plain on my snowshoes with bended knee
Where the thin wind stung my cheeks,
And the hard snow ran in little ripples and peaks,
Like the fretted floor of a white and petrified sea.

And a strange peace gathered about my soul and shone
As I sat reflecting there,
In a world so mystically fair,
So deathly silent – I so utterly alone.

Personality

O differing human heart,
Why is it that I tremble when thine eyes,
Thy human eyes and beautiful human speech,
Draw me, and stir within my soul
That subtle ineradicable longing
For tender friendship?
It is because I cannot all at once,
Through the half-lights and phantom-haunted mists
That separate and enshroud us from life,
Discern the nearness or the strangeness of thy paths,
Nor plumb thy depths.
I am like one that comes alone at night

To a strange stream, and by an unknown ford
Stands, and for a moment yearns and shrinks,
Being ignorant of the water, though so quiet it is,
So softly murmurous,
So silvered by the familiar moon.

BLISS CARMAN

1861–1929

Low Tide on Grand Pré

The sun goes down, and over all
  These barren reaches by the tide
Such unelusive glories fall,
  I almost dream they yet will bide
  Until the coming of the tide.

And yet I know that not for us,
  By any ecstasy of dream,
He lingers to keep luminous
  A little while the grievous stream,
  Which frets, uncomforted of dream –

A grievous stream, that to and fro
  Athrough the fields of Acadie
Goes wandering, as if to know
  Why one beloved face should be
  So long from home and Acadie.

Was it a year or lives ago
  We took the grasses in our hands,
And caught the summer flying low
  Over the waving meadow lands,
  And held it there between our hands?

The while the river at our feet –
  A drowsy inland meadow stream –
At set of sun the after-heat
  Made running gold, and in the gleam
  We freed our birch upon the stream.

There down along the elms at dusk
  We lifted dripping blade to drift,

Through twilight scented fine like musk,
  Where night and gloom awhile uplift,
  Nor sunder soul and soul adrift.

And that we took into our hands
  Spirit of life or subtler thing –
Breathed on us there, and loosed the bands
  Of death, and taught us, whispering,
  The secret of some wonder-thing.

Then all your face grew light, and seemed
  To hold the shadow of the sun;
The evening faltered, and I deemed
  That time was ripe, and years had done
  Their wheeling underneath the sun.

So all desire and all regret,
  And fear and memory, were naught;
One to remember or forget
  The keen delight our hands had caught;
  Morrow and yesterday were naught.

The night has fallen, and the tide . . .
  Now and again comes drifting home,
Across these aching barrens wide,
  A sigh like driven wind or foam:
  In grief the flood is bursting home.

A Northern Vigil

Here by the gray north sea,
  In the wintry heart of the wild,
Comes the old dream of thee,
  Guendolen, mistress and child.

The heart of the forest grieves
  In the drift against my door;

A voice is under the eaves,
  A footfall on the floor.

Threshold, mirror and hall,
  Vacant and strangely aware,
Wait for their soul's recall
  With the dumb expectant air.

Here when the smouldering west
  Burns down into the sea,
I take no heed of rest
  And keep the watch for thee.

I sit by the fire and hear
  The restless wind go by,
On the long dirge and drear,
  Under the low bleak sky.

When day puts out to sea
  And night makes in for land,
There is no lock for thee,
  Each door awaits thy hand!

When night goes over the hill
  And dawn comes down the dale,
It's O for the wild sweet will
  That shall no more prevail!

When the zenith moon is round,
  And snow-wraiths gather and run,
And there is set no bound
  To love beneath the sun,

O wayward will, come near
  The old mad wilful way,
The soft mouth at my ear
  With words too sweet to say!

Come, for the night is cold,
The ghostly moonlight fills
Hollow and rift and fold
Of the eerie Ardise hills!

The windows of my room
Are dark with bitter frost,
The stillness aches with doom
Of something loved and lost.

Outside, the great blue star
Burns in the ghostland pale,
Where giant Algebar
Holds on the endless trail.

Come, for the years are long,
And silence keeps the door,
Where shapes with the shadows throng
The firelit chamber floor.

Come, for thy kiss was warm,
With the red embers' glare
Across thy folding arm
And dark tumultuous hair!

And though thy coming rouse
The sleep-cry of no bird,
The keepers of the house
Shall tremble at thy word.

Come, for the soul is free!
In all the vast dreamland
There is no lock for thee,
Each door awaits thy hand.

Ah, not in dreams at all,
Fleering, perishing, dim,
But thy old self, supple and tall,
Mistress and child of whim!

The proud imperious guise,
  Impetuous and serene,
The sad mysterious eyes,
  And dignity of mien!

Yea, wilt thou not return,
  When the late hill-winds veer,
And the bright hill-flowers burn
  With the reviving year?

When April comes, and the sea
  Sparkles as if it smiled,
Will they restore to me
  My dark Love, empress and child?

The curtains seem to part;
  A sound is on the stair,
As if at the last . . . I start;
  Only the wind is there.

Lo, now far on the hills
  The crimson fumes uncurled,
Where the caldron mantles and spills
  Another dawn on the world!

A Seamark

A Threnody for Robert Louis Stevenson

Cold, the dull cold! What ails the sun,
And takes the heart out of the day?
What makes the morning look so mean,
The Common so forlorn and gray?

The wintry city's granite heart
Beats on in iron mockery,
And like the roaming mountain rains,
I hear the thresh of feet go by.

It is the lonely human surf
Surging through alleys chill with grime,
The muttering churning ceaseless floe
Adrift out of the North of time.

Fades, it all fades! I only see
The poster with its reds and blues
Bidding the heart stand still to take
Its desolating stab of news.

That intimate and magic name:
'Dead in Samoa.' . . . Cry your cries,
O city of the golden dome,
Under the gray Atlantic skies!

But I have wander-biddings now.
Far down the latitudes of sun,
An island mountain of the sea,
Piercing the green and rosy zone,

Goes up into the wondrous day.
And there the brown-limbed island men
Are bearing up for burial,
Within the sun's departing ken,

The master of the roving kind.
And there where time will set no mark
For his irrevocable rest,
Under the spacious melting dark,

With all the nomad tented stars
About him, they have laid him down
Above the crumbling of the sea,
Beyond the turmoil of renown.

O all you hearts about the world
In whom the truant gipsy blood,
Under the frost of this pale time,
Sleeps like the daring sap and flood

That dream of April and reprieve!
You whom the haunted vision drives,
Incredulous of home and ease,
Perfection's lovers all your lives!

You whom the wander-spirit loves
To lead by some forgotten clue
Forever vanishing beyond
Horizon brinks forever new;

The road, unmarked, ordained, whereby
Your brothers of the field and air
Before you, faithful, blind and glad,
Emerged from chaos pair by pair;

The road whereby you too must come,
In the unvexed and fabled years
Into the country of your dream,
With all your knowledge in arrears!

You who can never quite forget
Your glimpse of Beauty as she passed,
The well-head where her knee was pressed,
The dew wherein her foot was cast;

O you who bid the paint and clay
Be glorious when you are dead,
And fit the plangent words in rhyme
Where the dark secret lurks unsaid;

You brethren of the light-heart guild,
The mystic fellowcraft of joy,
Who tarry for the news of truth,
And listen for some vast ahoy

Blown in from sea, who crowd the wharves
With eager eyes that wait the ship
Whose foreign tongue may fill the world
With wondrous tales from lip to lip;

Our restless loved adventurer,
On secret orders come to him,
Has slipped his cable, cleared the reef,
And melted on the white sea-rim.

O granite hills, go down in blue!
And like green clouds in opal calms,
You anchored islands of the main,
Float up your loom of feathery palms!

For deep within your dales, where lies
A valiant earthling stark and dumb,
This savage undiscerning heart
Is with the silent chiefs who come

To mourn their kin and bear him gifts, –
Who kiss his hand, and take their place,
This last night he receives his friends,
The journey-wonder on his face.

He 'was not born for age'. Ah no,
For everlasting youth is his!
Part of the lyric of the earth
With spring and leaf and blade he is.

'Twill nevermore be April now
But there will lurk a thought of him
At the street corners, gay with flowers
From rainy valleys purple-dim.

O chiefs, you do not mourn alone!
In that stern North where mystery broods,
Our mother grief has many sons
Bred in those iron solitudes.

It does not help them, to have laid
Their coil of lightning under seas;
They are as impotent as you
To mend the loosened wrists and knees.

And yet how many a harvest night,
When the great luminous meteors flare
Along the trenches of the dusk,
The men who dwell beneath the Bear,

Seeing those vagrants of the sky
Float through the deep beyond their hark,
Like Arabs through the wastes of air, –
A flash, a dream, from dark to dark, –

Must feel the solemn large surmise:
By a dim vast and perilous way
We sweep through undetermined time,
Illumining this quench of clay,

A moment staunched, then forth again.
Ah, not alone you climb the steep
To set your loving burden down
Against the mighty knees of sleep.

With you we hold the sombre faith
Where creeds are sown like rain at sea;
And leave the loveliest child of earth
To slumber where he longed to be.

His fathers lit the dangerous coast
To steer the daring merchant home;
His courage lights the dark'ning port
Where every sea-worn sail must come.

And since he was the type of all
That strain in us which still must fare,
The fleeting migrant of a day,
Heart-high, outbound for otherwhere,

Now therefore, where the passing ships
Hang on the edges of the noon,
And Northern liners trail their smoke
Across the rising yellow moon,

Bound for his home, with shuddering screw
That beats its strength out into speed,
Until the pacing watch descries
On the sea-line a scarlet seed

Smolder and kindle and set fire
To the dark selvedge of the night,
The deep blue tapestry of stars,
Then sheet the dome in pearly light,

There in perpetual tides of day,
Where men may praise him and deplore,
The place of his lone grave shall be
A seamark set forevermore,

High on a peak adrift with mist,
And round whose bases, far beneath
The snow-white wheeling tropic birds,
The emerald dragon breaks his teeth.

Christmas Song

Above the weary waiting world,
Asleep in chill despair,
There breaks a sound of joyous bells
Upon the frosted air.
And o'er the humblest rooftree, lo,
A star is dancing on the snow.

What makes the yellow star to dance
Upon the brink of night?
What makes the breaking dawn to glow
So magically bright, –
And all the earth to be renewed
With infinite beatitude?

The singing bells, the throbbing star,
The sunbeams on the snow,
And the awakening heart that leaps
New ecstasy to know, –
They all are dancing in the morn
Because a little child is born.

From *Sappho*

XCIII

When in the spring the swallows all return,
And the bleak bitter sea grows mild once more
With all its thunders softened to a sigh;

When to the meadows the young green comes back,
And swelling buds put forth on every bough,
With wild-wood odours on the delicate air;

Ah, then, in that so lovely earth wilt thou
With all thy beauty love me all one way,
And make me all thy lover as before?

Lo, where the white-maned horses of the surge,
Plunging in thunderous onset to the shore,
Trample and break and charge along the sand!

FREDERICK GEORGE SCOTT

1861–1944

The Sting of Death

'Is Sin, then, fair?'
Nay, love, come now,
Put back the hair
From his sunny brow;
See, here, blood-red
Across his head
A brand is set,
The word – 'Regret.'

'Is Sin so fleet
That while he stays,
Our hands and feet
May go his ways?'
Nay, love, his breath
Clings round like death,
He slakes desire
With liquid fire.

'Is Sin Death's sting?'
Ay, sure he is,
His golden wing
Darkens man's bliss;
And when Death comes,
Sin sits and hums
A chaunt of fears
Into man's ears.

'How slayeth Sin?'
First, God is hid,
And the heart within
By its own self chid;

Then the maddened brain
Is scourged by pain
To sin as before
And more and more,
For evermore.

The Snowstorm

The sky is hid in a snowy shroud,
And the road in the woods is white,
But the dear God watches above the cloud
In the centre of light.

In the woods is the hush of the snowflakes' fall,
And the creak of a lumberman's sleigh,
But in Heaven the choirs of the Master of all
Make praise alway.

Up there is the throne of the Triune God
And the worshipping multitudes,
And here is the long white winter road
And the silent woods.

'Te Judice'

Dost thou deem that thyself
Art as white from sin
As a platter of delf, –
Outside and in?
When thine eyes behold
Christ's kind face lean
From His throne of gold
To test what is told
Of the life that hath been,

Like a leper of old,
    Thou wilt cry, 'Unclean!
    Unclean! Unclean!'

And thinkest thou this –
    That thou judgest aright
Thy heart as it is
    In God's and man's sight?
Fool, take up thy light,
And descend the stair steep
To thy heart's dungeons deep,
And search them and sweep
    Till their ghosts are unmasked;
Else, when judgment is come,
Thou wilt stand stark and dumb
    At the first question asked.

DUNCAN CAMPBELL SCOTT

1862–1947

The Piper of Arll

There was in Arll a little cove
Where the salt wind came cool and free:
A foamy beach that one would love,
If he were longing for the sea.

A brook hung sparkling on the hill,
The hill swept far to ring the bay;
The bay was faithful, wild or still,
To the heart of the ocean far away.

There were three pines above the comb
That, when the sun flared and went down,
Grew like three warriors reaving home
The plunder of a burning town.

A piper lived within the grove,
Tending the pasture of his sheep;
His heart was swayed with faithful love,
From the springs of God's ocean clear and deep.

And there a ship one evening stood,
Where ship had never stood before;
A pennon bickered red as blood,
An angel glimmered at the prore.

About the coming on of dew,
The sails burned rosy, and the spars
Were gold, and all the tackle grew
Alive with ruby-hearted stars.

The piper heard an outland tongue,
With music in the cadenced fall;

And when the fairy lights were hung,
The sailors gathered one and all,

And leaning on the gunwales dark,
Crusted with shells and dashed with foam,
With all the dreaming hills to hark,
They sang their longing songs of home.

When the sweet airs had fled away,
The piper, with a gentle breath,
Moulded a tranquil melody
Of lonely love and long-for death.

When the fair sound began to lull,
From out the fireflies and the dew,
A silence held the shadowy hull,
Until the eerie tune was through.

Then from the dark and dreamy deck
An alien song began to thrill;
It mingled with the drumming beck,
And stirred the braird upon the hill.

Beneath the stars each sent to each
A message tender, till at last
The piper slept upon the beach,
The sailors slumbered round the mast.

Still as a dream till nearly dawn,
The ship was bosomed on the tide;
The streamlet, murmuring on and on,
Bore the sweet water to her side.

Then shaking out her lawny sails,
Forth on the misty sea she crept;
She left the dawning of the dales,
Yet in his cloak the piper slept.

And when he woke he saw the ship,
Limned black against the crimson sun;

Then from the disc he saw her slip,
A wraith of shadow – she was gone.

He threw his mantle on the beach,
He went apart like one distraught,
His lips were moved – his desperate speech
Stormed his inviolable thought.

He broke his human-throated reed,
And threw it in the idle rill;
But when his passion had its mead,
He found it in the eddy still.

He mended well the patient flue,
Again he tried its varied stops;
The closures answered right and true,
And starting out in piercing drops,

A melody began to drip
That mingled with a ghostly thrill
The vision-spirit of the ship,
The secret of his broken will.

Beneath the pines he piped and swayed,
Master of passion and of power;
He was his soul and what he played,
Immortal for a happy hour.

He, singing into nature's heart,
Guiding his will by the world's will,
With deep, unconscious, childlike art
Had sung his soul out and was still.

And then at evening came the bark
That stirred his dreaming heart's desire;
It burned slow lights along the dark
That died in glooms of crimson fire.

The sailors launched a sombre boat,
And bent with music at the oars;
The rhythm throbbing every throat,
And lapsing round the liquid shores,

Was that true tune the piper sent,
Unto the wave-worn mariners,
When with the beck and ripple blent
He heard that outland song of theirs.

Silent they rowed him, dip and drip,
The oars beat out an exequy,
They laid him down within the ship,
They loosed a rocket to the sky.

It broke in many a crimson sphere
That grew to gold and floated far,
And left the sudden shore-line clear,
With one slow-changing, drifting star.

Then out they shook the magic sails,
That charmed the wind in other seas,
From where the west line pearls and pales,
They waited for a ruffling breeze.

But in the world there was no stir,
The cordage slacked with never a creak,
They heard the flame begin to purr
Within the lantern at the peak.

They could not cry, they could not move,
They felt the lure from the charmed sea;
They could not think of home or love
Or any pleasant land to be.

They felt the vessel dip and trim,
And settle down from list to list;
They saw the sea-plain heave and swim
As gently as a rising mist.

And down so slowly, down and down,
Rivet by rivet, plank by plank;
A little flood of ocean flown
Across the deck, she sank and sank.

From knee to breast the water wore,
It crept and crept; ere they were ware
Gone was the angel at the prore,
They felt the water float their hair.

They saw the salt plain spark and shine,
They threw their faces to the sky;
Beneath a deepening film of brine
They saw the star-flash blur and die.

She sank and sank by yard and mast,
Sank down the shimmering gradual dark;
A little drooping pennon last
Showed like the black fin of a shark.

And down she sank till, keeled in sand,
She rested safely balanced true,
With all her upward gazing band,
The piper and the dreaming crew.

And there, unmarked of any chart,
In unrecorded deeps they lie,
Empearled within the purple heart
Of the great sea for aye and aye.

Their eyes are ruby in the green
Long shaft of sun that spreads and rays,
And upward with a wizard sheen
A fan of sea-light leaps and plays.

Tendrils of or and azure creep,
And globes of amber light are rolled,

And in the gloaming of the deep
Their eyes are starry pits of gold.

And sometimes in the liquid night
The hull is changed, a solid gem,
That glows with a soft stony light,
The lost prince of a diadem.

And at the keel a vine is quick,
That spreads its bines and works and weaves
O'er all the timbers veining thick
A plenitude of silver leaves.

Thoughts

These thoughts of mine
Oh! would they were away.
Thoughts that have progress
Give me stay
And eagerness for life;
But these dead thoughts
Hang like burned forests
By a northern lake,
Whose waters take
The bone-grey skeletons
And mirror the grey bones,
Both dead, the trees and the reflections.

Compare these thoughts
To anything that nothing tells, –
To toads alive for centuries in stone cells,
To a styleless dial on a fiery lawn,
To the trapped bride within the oaken chest,
Or to the dull, intolerable bells
That beat the dawn
And will not let us rest!

Watkwenies

Vengeance was once her nation's lore and law:
When the tired sentry stooped above the rill,
Her long knife flashed, and hissed, and drank its fill;
Dimly below her dripping wrist she saw
One wild hand, pale as death and weak as straw,
Clutch at the ripple in the pool; while shrill
Sprang through the dreaming hamlet on the hill,
The war-cry of the triumphant Iroquois.

Now clothed with many an ancient flap and fold,
And wrinkled like an apple kept till May,
She weighs the interest-money in her palm,
And, when the Agent calls her valiant name,
Hears, like the war-whoops of her perished day,
The lads playing snow-snake in the stinging cold.

The Onondaga Madonna

She stands full-throated and with careless pose,
This woman of a weird and waning race,
The tragic savage lurking in her face,
Where all her pagan passion burns and glows;
Her blood is mingled with her ancient foes,
And thrills with war and wildness in her veins;
Her rebel lips are dabbled with the stains
Of feuds and forays and her father's woes.

And closer in the shawl about her breast,
The latest promise of her nation's doom,
Paler than she her baby clings and lies,
The primal warrior gleaming from his eyes;
He sulks, and burdened with his infant gloom,
He draws his heavy brows and will not rest.

The Sailor's Sweetheart

O if love were had for asking
   In the markets of the town,
Hardly a lass would think to wear
   A fine silken gown:
But love is had by grieving
By choosing and by leaving,
And there's no one now to ask me
If heavy lies my heart.

O if love were had for a deep wish
   In the deadness of the night,
There'd be a truce to longing
   Between the dusk and the light:
But love is had for sighing,
For living and for dying,
And there's no one now to ask me
If heavy lies my heart.

O if love were had for taking
   Like honey from the hive,
The bees that made the tender stuff
   Could hardly keep alive:
But love it is a wounded thing,
A tremor and a smart,
And there's no one left to kiss me now
Over my heavy heart.

A Song

In the air there are no coral-
   Reefs or ambergris,
No rock-pools that hide the lovely
   Sea-anemones,
No strange forms that flow with phosphor
   In a deep-sea night,

No slow fish that float their colour
Through the liquid light,
No young pearls, like new moons, growing
Perfect in their shells;
If you be in search of beauty
Go where beauty dwells.

In the sea there are no sunsets
Crimson in the west,
No dark pines that hold the shadow
On the mountain-crest,
There is neither mist nor moonrise
Rainbows nor rain,
No sweet flowers that in the autumn
Die to bloom again,
Music never moves the silence, –
Reeds or silver bells;
If you be in search of beauty
Go where beauty dwells.

At Delos

An iris-flower with topaz leaves,
With a dark heart of deeper gold,
Died over Delos when light failed
And the night grew cold.

No wave fell mourning in the sea
Where age on age beauty had died;
For that frail colour withering away
No sea-bird cried.

There is no grieving in the world
As beauty fades throughout the years:
The pilgrim with the weary heart
Brings to the grave his tears.

TOM MacINNES

1867–1951

Zalinka

1

Last night in a land of triangles,
  I lay in a cubicle, where
A girl in pyjamas and bangles
  Slept with her hands in my hair.

2

I wondered if either or neither
  Of us were properly there,
Being subject to queer aberrations –
Astral and thin aberrations –
  Which leave me no base to compare:
  No adequate base to compare:
Tho' her hands, with their wristful of bangles,
  Were certainly fast in my hair,
While the moon made pallid equations
  Thro' a delicate window there.

3

I was glad that she slept for I never
  Can tell what the finish will be:
What enamoured, nocturnal endeavour
  May end in the killing of me:
But, in the moonlit obscuro
  Of that silken, somniferous lair,
Like a poet consumed with a far lust
  Of things unapproachably fair
I fancied her body of stardust –
Pounded of spices and stardust –
  Out of the opulent air.

4

Then the moon, with its pale liquidations,
  Fell across her in argentine bars,
And I thought: This is fine – but to-morrow
  What cut of Dawn's cold scimitars
Will sever my hold on this creature –
  I mean of this creature on me? –
Amorous creature of exquisite aura –
  Marvel of dark glamorie.

5

What joy of folly then followed
  Is beyond my expression in rhyme:
And I do not expect you to grasp it
  When I speak of expansions of time:
Of reaching and zooming serenely
  As it were at right angles to time:
Knowing well you will think, on your level,
  This was only a dream indiscreet –
  Or experience quite indiscreet:
But little I care, in this instance,
  What you do or do not think discreet:
  O utterance futile, but sweet,
  Like a parrot I pause and repeat,
In delight of my own, and for nothing,
  To myself I repeat and repeat:

6

Last night in a land of triangles,
  I lay in a cubicle where
A girl in pyjamas and bangles
  Slept with her hands in my hair.

JOHN McCRAE

1872–1918

In Flanders Fields

In Flanders fields the poppies blow
Between the crosses, row on row,
  That mark our place; and in the sky
  The larks, still bravely singing, fly
Scarce heard amid the guns below.

We are the Dead. Short days ago
We lived, felt dawn, saw sunset glow,
  Loved and were loved, and now we lie,
      In Flanders fields.

Take up our quarrel with the foe:
To you from failing hands we throw
  The torch; be yours to hold it high.
  If ye break faith with us who die
We shall not sleep, though poppies grow
      In Flanders fields.

VIRNA SHEARD

d. 1943

The Yak

For hours the princess would not play or sleep
 Or take the air;
Her red mouth wore a look it meant to keep
 Unmelted there;
(Each tired courtier longed to shriek, or weep,
 But did not dare.)

Then one young duchess said: 'I'll to the King,
 And short and flat
I'll say, "Her Highness will not play or sing
 Or pet the cat;
Or feed the peacocks, or do anything –
 And that is that." '

So to the King she went, curtsied, and said,
 (No whit confused):
'Your Majesty, I would go home! The court is dead.
 Have me excused;
The little princess still declines,' – she tossed her head –
 'To be amused.'

Then to the princess stalked the King: 'What ho!' he roared,
 'What may you lack?
Why do you look, my love, so dull and bored
 With all this pack
Of minions?' She answered, while he waved his sword:
 'I want a yak.'

'A yak!' he cried (each courtier cried, 'Yak! Yak!'
 As at a blow)
'Is that a figure on the zodiac?
 Or horse? Or crow?'

The princess sadly said to him: 'Alack
I do not know.'

'We'll send the vassals far and wide, my dear!'
Then quoth the King:
'They'll make a hunt for it, then come back here
And bring the thing; –
But warily, – lest it be wild, or queer,
Or have a sting.'

So off the vassals went, and well they sought
On every track,
Till by and by in old Tibet they bought
An ancient yak.
Yet when the princess saw it, she said naught
But: 'Take it back!'

And what the courtiers thought they did not say
(Save soft and low),
For that is surely far the wisest way
As we all know;
While for the princess? She went back to play!
Tra-rill-a-la-lo!
Tra-rill-a-la-lo!
Tra-rill-a-la-lo!

Exile

Ben-Arabie was the Camel,
Belonging to the Zoo.
He lived there through a dozen years,
With nothing much to do,
But chew, and chew, and chew, and chew,
And chew, and chew, and chew.

He wondered when he might go home, –
And what they kept him for;

Because he hated Zooish sounds
And perfumes – more and more; –
Decidedly he hated them
Much more, and more, and more.

And why the world turned white and cold
He did not understand.
He only wanted lots of sun
And lots and lots of sand;
Just sand, and sand, and sand, and sand,
And sand, and sand, and sand.

He longed to see an Arab Sheik,
And Arab girls and boys;
The kind of noise he yearned for most
Was plain Arabian noise;
(The sound of little drums and flutes
And all that sort of noise.)

He leant against the wind to hear
The sound of harness bells;
He sniffed the air for scent of spice
The nomad merchant sells;
He dreamed of pleasant tinkling bells,
Of spice and tinkling bells.

The keepers said that he grew queer.
They wondered why he sighed;
They called him supercilious
And crabbed and sun-dried;
(Indeed he was quite crabbed and
Exceedingly sun-dried.)

But ere his woolly fur was gone
They put him on a train –
For a rich old Arab bought him
And sent him home again; –
O joyous day! He sent him home;
He sent him home again!

THEODORE GOODRIDGE ROBERTS

1877–1953

The Blue Heron

In a green place lanced through
With amber and gold and blue;
A place of water and weeds
And roses pinker than dawn,
And ranks of lush young reeds,
And grasses straightly withdrawn
From graven ripples of sands,
The still blue heron stands.

Smoke-blue he is, and grey
As embers of yesterday.
Still he is, as death;
Like stone, or shadow of stone,
Without a pulse or breath,
Motionless and alone
There in the lily stems:
But his eyes are alive like gems.

Still as a shadow; still
Grey feather and yellow bill:
Still as an image made
Of mist and smoke half hid
By windless sunshine and shade,
Save when a yellow lid
Slides and is gone like a breath:
Death-still – and sudden as death!

The Wreckers' Prayer

In the old days before the building of the lighthouses, the poor 'noddies' of many a Newfoundland outport prayed for wrecks – aye, and with easy consciences. Only the few hundreds of them who took to deep-sea voyaging ever learned anything of the world and its peoples. All the world excepting their own desolate bays and 'down Nort' ', was 'up-along' to them . . . a grand, rich place where all men were gentlemen wearing collars and coats, eating figgy-duff every day and smoking all they wanted to. The folk of up-along had the easy end of life; so why shouldn't they contribute something of their goods and gear to poor but honest noddies now and then, even if against their inclinations – aye, even if at the cost of their lives?

Give us a wrack or two, Good Lard,
For winter in Tops'il Tickle bes hard,
Wid grey frost creepin' like mortal sin
And perishin' lack of bread in the bin.

A grand, rich wrack, us do humbly pray,
Busted abroad at the break o' day
An' hove clear in 'crost Tops'il Reef,
Wid victuals an' gear to beguile our grief.

God of reefs an' tides an' sky,
Heed Ye our need an' hark to our cry!
Bread by the bag an' beef by the cask.
Ease for sore bellies bes all we ask.

One grand wrack – or maybe two? –
Wid gear an' victuals to see us through
'Til Spring starts up like the leap of day
An' the fish strike back into Tops'il Bay.

One rich wrack – for Thy hand bes strong!
A barque or a brig from up-along
Bemused by Thy twisty tides, O Lard!
For winter in Tops'il Tickle bes hard.

Loud an' long will us sing Yer praise,
Marciful Fadder, O Ancient of Days,
Master of fog an' tide an' reef!
Heave us a wrack to beguile our grief. Amen.

MARJORIE PICKTHALL

1883–1922

Père Lalement

I lift the Lord on high,
Under the murmuring hemlock boughs, and see
The small birds of the forest lingering by
And making melody.
These are mine acolytes and these my choir,
And this mine altar in the cool green shade,
Where the wild soft-eyed does draw nigh
Wondering, as in the byre
Of Bethlehem the oxen heard Thy cry
And saw Thee, unafraid.

My boatmen sit apart,
Wolf-eyed, wolf-sinewed, stiller than the trees.
Help me, O Lord, for very slow of heart
And hard of faith are these.
Cruel are they, yet Thy children. Foul are they,
Yet wert Thou born to save them utterly.
Then make me as I pray
Just to their hates, kind to their sorrows, wise
After their speech, and strong before their free
Indomitable eyes.

Do the French lilies reign
Over Mont Royal and Stadacona still?
Up the St Lawrence comes the spring again,
Crowning each southward hill
And blossoming pool with beauty, while I roam
Far from the perilous folds that are my home,
There where we built St Ignace for our needs,
Shaped the rough roof tree, turned the first sweet sod,
St Ignace and St Louis, little beads
On the rosary of God.

Pines shall Thy pillars be,
Fairer than those Sidonian cedars brought
By Hiram out of Tyre, and each birch-tree
Shines like a holy thought.
But come no worshippers; shall I confess,
St Francis-like, the birds of the wilderness?
O, with Thy love my lonely head uphold.
A wandering shepherd I, who hath no sheep;
A wandering soul, who hath no scrip, nor gold,
Nor anywhere to sleep.

My hour of rest is done;
On the smooth ripple lifts the long canoe;
The hemlocks murmur sadly as the sun
Slants his dim arrows through.
Whither I go I know not, nor the way,
Dark with strange passions, vexed with heathen charms,
Holding I know not what of life or death;
Only be Thou beside me day by day,
Thy rod my guide and comfort, underneath
Thy everlasting arms.

Mary Tired

Through the starred Judean night
  She went in travail of the Light:
  With the earliest hush she saw
God beside her in the straw.
One small taper glimmered clear,
  Drowsing Joseph nodded near;
All the glooms were rosed with wings.
She that knew the Spirit's kiss
Wearied of the bright abyss.
She was tired of heavenly things.
There between the day and night
These she counted for delight:

Baby kids that butted hard
In the shadowy stable yard;
Silken doves that dipped and preened
Where the crumbling well-curb greened;
Sparrows in the vine, and small
Sapphired flies upon the wall,
So lovely they seemed musical.
In the roof a swallow built;
All the newborn airs were spilt
Out of cups the morning made
Of a glory and a shade.
These her solemn eyelids felt,
While unseen the seraphs knelt.
Then a young mouse, sleek and bold,
Rustling in the winnowed gold,
To her shadow crept, and curled
Near the Ransom of the World.

On Amaryllis
A Tortoyse

My name was Amaryllis. I
From a harde Shell put forthe to fly;
No Bird, alas! with Beautie prim'd,
Hath Death th' inconstant Fowler lim'd.
No antick Moth on blossoms set
Hath Judgement taken in a Net.
So dull, so slowe, so meeke I went
In my House-Roof that pay'd no Rent,
E'en my deare Mistresse guess'd no Spark
Could e'er enlight'n my dustie Dark.
Judge not, ye Proud. Each lowlie Thing
May lack the Voyce, not Heart, to sing.
The Worme that from the Moulde suspires
May be attun'd with heavenlie Quires,
And I, a-crawling in my Straw,
Was moved by Love, and made by Law.

So all ye wise, who 'neath your Clod
Go creeping onwards up to God,
Take Heart of me, who by His Grace,
Slough'd off my Pris'n and won my Race.

E. J. PRATT

1883–1964

Come Away, Death

Willy-nilly, he comes or goes, with the clown's logic,
Comic in epitaph, tragic in epithalamium,
And unseduced by any mused rhyme.
However blow the winds over the pollen,
Whatever the course of the garden variables,
He remains the constant,
Ever flowering from the poppy seeds.

There was a time he came in formal dress,
Announced by Silence tapping at the panels
In deep apology.
A touch of chivalry in his approach,
He offered sacramental wine,
And with acanthus leaf
And petals of the hyacinth
He took the fever from the temples
And closed the eyelids,
Then led the way to his cool longitudes
In the dignity of the candles.

His mediaeval grace is gone –
Gone with the flame of the capitals
And the leisured turn of the thumb
Leafing the manuscripts,
Gone with the marbles
And the Venetian mosaics,
With the bend of the knee
Before the rose-strewn feet of the Virgin.
The *paternosters* of his priests,
Committing clay to clay,
Have rattled in their throats
Under the gride of his traction tread.

One night we heard his footfall – one September night –
In the outskirts of a village near the sea.
There was a moment when the storm
Delayed its fist, when the surf fell
Like velvet on the rocks – a moment only;
The strangest lull we ever knew!
A sudden truce among the oaks
Released their fratricidal arms;
The poplars straightened to attention
As the winds stopped to listen
To the sound of a motor drone –
And then the drone was still.
We heard the tick-tock on the shelf,
And the leak of valves in our hearts.
A calm condensed and lidded
As at the core of a cyclone ended breathing.
This was the monologue of Silence
Grave and unequivocal.

What followed was a bolt
Outside the range and target of the thunder,
And human speech curved back upon itself
Through Druid runways and the Piltdown scarps,
Beyond the stammers of the Java caves,
To find its origins in hieroglyphs
On mouths and eyes and cheeks
Etched by a foreign stylus never used
On the outmoded page of the Apocalypse.

From *Brébeuf and His Brethren*

The fury of taunt was followed by fury of blow.
Why did not the flesh of Brébeuf cringe to the scourge,
Respond to the heat, for rarely the Iroquois found
A victim that would not cry out in such pain – yet here
The fire was on the wrong fuel. Whenever he spoke,
It was to rally the soul of his friend whose turn

Was to come through the night while the eyes were uplifted in
prayer,
Imploring the Lady of Sorrows, the mother of Christ,
As pain brimmed over the cup and the will was called
To stand the test of the coals. And sometimes the speech
Of Brébeuf struck out, thundering reproof to his foes,
Half-rebuke, half-defiance, giving them roar for roar.
Was it because the chancel became the arena,
Brébeuf a lion at bay, not a lamb on the altar,
As if the might of a Roman were joined to the cause
Of Judaea? Speech they could stop for they girdled his lips,
But never a moan could they get. Where was the source
Of his strength, the home of his courage that topped the best
Of their braves and even out-fabled the lore of their legends?
In the bunch of his shoulders which often had carried a load
Extorting the envy of guides at an Ottawa portage?
The heat of the hatchets was finding a path to that source.
In the thews of his thighs which had mastered the trails of the
Neutrals?
They would gash and beribbon those muscles. Was it the blood?
They would draw it fresh from its fountain. Was it the heart?
They dug for it, fought for the scraps in the way of the wolves.
But not in these was the valour or stamina lodged;
Nor in the symbol of Richelieu's robes or the seals
Of Mazarin's charters, nor in the stir of the *lilies*
Upon the Imperial folds; nor yet in the words
Loyola wrote on a table of lava-stone
In the cave of Manresa – not in these the source –
But in the sound of invisible trumpets blowing
Around two slabs of board, right-angled, hammered
By Roman nails and hung on a Jewish hill.

From *The Titanic*

Out on the water was the same display
Of fear and self-control as on the deck –
Challenge and hesitation and delay,

The quick return, the will to save, the race
Of snapping oars to put the realm of space
Between the half-filled lifeboats and the wreck.

... Aboard the ship, whatever hope of dawn
Gleamed from the *Carpathia*'s riding lights was gone,
For every knot was matched by each degree
Of list. The stern was lifted bodily
When the bow had sunk three hundred feet, and set
Against the horizon stars in silhouette
Were the blade curves of the screws, hump of the rudder.
The downward pull and after buoyancy
Held her a minute poised but for a shudder
That caught her frame as with the upward stroke
Of the sea a boiler or a bulkhead broke.

Climbing the ladders, gripping shroud and stay,
Storm-rail, ringbolt or fairlead, every place
That might befriend the clutch of hand or brace
Of foot, the fourteen hundred made their way
To the heights of the aft decks, crowding the inches
Around the docking bridge and cargo winches.
And now that last salt tonic which had kept
The valour of the heart alive – the bows
Of the immortal seven that had swept
The strings to outplay, outdie their orders, ceased.
Five minutes more, the angle had increased
From eighty on to ninety when the rows
Of deck and porthole lights went out, flashed back
A brilliant second and again went black.
Another bulkhead crashed, then following
The passage of the engines as they tore
From their foundations, taking everything
Clean through the bows from 'midships with a roar
Which drowned all cries upon the deck and shook
The watchers in the boats, the liner took
Her thousand fathoms journey to her grave.

* * *

And out there in the starlight, with no trace
Upon it of its deed but the last wave
From the *Titanic* fretting at its base,
Silent, composed, ringed by its icy broods,
The gray shape with the palaeolithic face
Was still the master of the longitudes.

The Prize Cat

Pure blood domestic, guaranteed,
Soft-mannered, musical in purr,
The ribbon had declared the breed,
Gentility was in the fur.

Such feline culture in the gads,
No anger ever arched her back –
What distance since those velvet pads
Departed from the leopard's track!

And when I mused how Time had thinned
The jungle strains within the cells,
How human hands had disciplined
Those prowling optic parallels;

I saw the generations pass
Along the reflex of a spring,
A bird had rustled in the grass,
The tab had caught it on the wing:

Behind the leap so furtive-wild
Was such ignition in the gleam,
I thought an Abyssinian child
Had cried out in the whitethroat's scream.

From Stone to Steel

From stone to bronze, from bronze to steel
Along the road-dust of the sun,

Two revolutions of the wheel
From Java to Geneva run.

The snarl Neanderthal is worn
Close to the smiling Aryan lips,
The civil polish of the horn
Gleams from our praying finger tips.

The evolution of desire
Has but matured a toxic wine,
Drunk long before its heady fire
Reddened Euphrates or the Rhine.

Between the temple and the cave
The boundary lies tissue-thin:
The yearlings still the altars crave
As satisfaction for a sin.

The road goes up, the road goes down –
Let Java or Geneva be –
But whether to the cross or crown,
The path lies through Gethsemane.

Come not the Seasons Here

Comes not the springtime here,
   Though the snowdrop came,
And the time of the cowslip is near,
   For a yellow flame
Was found in a tuft of green;
   And the joyous shout
   Of a child rang out
That a cuckoo's eggs were seen.

Comes not the summer here,
   Though the cowslip be gone,
Though the wild rose blow as the year
   Draws faithfully on;

Though the face of the poppy be red
 In the morning light,
 And the ground be white
With the bloom of the locust shed.

Comes not the autumn here,
 Though someone said
He found a leaf in the sere
 By an aster dead;
And knew that the summer was done,
 For a herdsman cried
That his pastures were brown in the sun,
 And his wells were dried.

Nor shall the winter come,
 Though the elm be bare,
And every voice be dumb
 On the frozen air;
But the flap of a waterfowl
 In the marsh alone,
Or the hoot of a horned owl
 On a glacial stone.

KENNETH LESLIE

1892–

Two Sonnets

From *By Stubborn Stars*

I

The silver herring throbbed thick in my seine,
silver of life, life's silver sheen of glory;
my hands, cut with the cold, hurt with the pain
of hauling the net, pulled the heavy dory,
heavy with life, low in the water, deep
plunged to the gunwale's lips in the stress of rowing,
the pulse of rowing that puts the world to sleep,
world within world endlessly ebbing, flowing.
At length you stood on the landing and you cried,
with quick low cries you timed me stroke on stroke
as I steadily won my way with the fulling tide
and crossed the threshold where the last wave broke
and coasted over the step of water and threw
straight through the air my mooring line to you.

II

A warm rain whispers, but the earth knows best
and turns a deaf ear, waiting for the snow,
the foam of bloom forgotten, the rolling crest
of green forgotten and the fruit swelling slow.
The shearing plow was here and cut the mould
and shouldered over the heavy rain-soaked lands,
letting the hot breath out for the quiet cold
to reach deep down with comfort in its hands.
The sap is ebbing from the tips of the trees
to the dry and secret heart, hiding away
from the blade still green with stubborn memories;
down in the roots it closes the door of clay
on grief and growing and this late warm rain
babbling false promises in the pasture lane.

W. W. E. ROSS

1894–1966

The Walk

He walked through the woods
and saw the merging
of the tall trunks
in the green distance, –
the undergrowth
of mottled green,
with sunlight and shadow,
and flowers starting

here and there
on the mottled ground;
he looked along
the green distance
and up towards
the greenly-laden
curving boughs
of the tall trees;

and down a slope,
as he walked onward
down the sloping
ground, he saw
in among
the green, broken,
the blue shimmering
of lake-water.

Fish

A fish dripping
sparkling drops

of crystal water,
pulled from the lake;
long has it dwelt
in the cool water,
in the cold water
of the lake.

Long has it wandered
to and fro
over the bottom
of the lake
among mysterious
recesses
there in the semi-
light of the water;

now to appear
surprised, aghast,
out of its element
into the day; –
out of the cold
and shining lake
the fish dripping
sparkling water.

The Diver

I would like to dive
Down
Into this still pool
Where the rocks at the bottom are safely deep,

Into the green
Of the water seen from within,
A strange light
Streaming past my eyes –

Things hostile,
You cannot stay here, they seem to say;
The rocks, slime-covered, the undulating
Fronds of weeds –

And drift slowly
Among the cooler zones;
Then, upward turning,
Break from the green glimmer

Into the light,
White and ordinary of the day,
And the mild air,
With the breeze and the comfortable shore.

'*The saws were shrieking*'

The saws were shrieking
and cutting into
the clean white wood
of the spruce logs
or the tinted hemlock
that smells as sweet –
or stronger pine,
the white and the red.

A whirling saw
received the logs;
the sound was ominous
and shrill,
rising above
the duller roaring
of the mill's
machinery.

From the revolving
of the saw

came slices of clear wood,
newly sawn,
white pine and red,
or spruce and hemlock,
the sweet spruce,
and the sweet hemlock.

In the Ravine

In the ravine   I stood
and watched the snowflakes
falling   into the stream
        into the stream
flowing gracefully between
banks of snow
                The black water
of the winter creek   came
around a bend   above
and disappeared
around a bend   below

Filled with melted snow
to the brim
the creek   came
around a bend –
and disappeared below
around a bend –
ground covered with snow

Thus I stood   the snow
descended   by degrees
into the stream
        into the stream

RAYMOND KNISTER

1899–1932

The Plowman

All day I follow
Watching the swift dark furrow
That curls away before me,
And care not for skies or upturned flowers,
And at the end of the field
Look backward
Ever with discontent.
A stone, a root, a strayed thought
Has warped the line of that furrow –
And urge my horses 'round again.

Sometimes even before the row is finished
I must look backward;
To find, when I come to the end
That there I swerved.

Unappeased I leave the field,
Expectant, return.

The horses are very patient.
When I tell myself
This time
The ultimate unflawed turning
Is before my share,
They must give up their rest.

Someday, someday, be sure,
I shall turn the furrow of all my hopes
But I shall not, doing it, look backward.

Feed

For Danny whistling slowly
'Down in Tennessee'
A fat white shoat by the trough
Lifts his snout a moment to hear,
Among the guzzling and slavering comrades,
Squeezing and forcing:
And begins to feed again.
Whenever the certain note comes
He will raise his jaws
With his unturning eyes,
Then lean again to scoop up the swill.

Lake Harvest

Down on the flat of the lake
Out on the slate and the green,
Spotting the border of Erie's sleeping robe of silver-blue changeable silk,
In sight of the shimmer of silver-blue changeable silk,
In the sun,
The men are sawing the frosted crystal.
Patient the horses look on from the sleighs,
Patient the trees, down from the bank, darkly ignoring the sun.
Each saw sings and whines in a grey-mittened hand,
And diamonds and pieces of a hundred rainbows are strown around.

Change

I shall not wonder more, then,
But I shall know.

Leaves change, and birds, flowers,
And after years are still the same.

The sea's breast heaves in sighs to the moon,
But they are moon and sea forever.

As in other times the trees stand tense and lonely,
And spread a hollow moan of other times.

You will be you yourself,
I'll find you more, not else,
For vintage of the woeful years.

The sea breathes, or broods, or loudens,
Is bright or is mist and the end of the world;
And the sea is constant to change.

I shall not wonder more, then,
But I shall know.

F. R. SCOTT

1899–

Trans Canada

Pulled from our ruts by the made-to-order gale
We sprang upward into a wider prairie
And dropped Regina below like a pile of bones.

Sky tumbled upon us in waterfalls,
But we were smarter than a Skeena salmon
And shot our silver body over the lip of air
To rest in a pool of space
On the top storey of our adventure.

A solar peace
And a six-way choice.

Clouds, now, are the solid substance,
A floor of wool roughed by the wind
Standing in waves that halt in their fall.
A still of troughs.

The plane, our planet,
Travels on roads that are not seen or laid
But sound in instruments on pilots' ears,
While underneath,
The sure wings
Are the everlasting arms of science.

Man, the lofty worm, tunnels his latest clay,
And bores his new career.

This frontier, too, is ours.
This everywhere whose life can only be led
At the pace of a rocket
Is common to man and man,
And every country below is an I land.

The sun sets on its top shelf,
And stars seem farther from our nearer grasp.
I have sat by nights beside a cold lake
And touched things smoother than moonlight on still water,
But the moon on this cloud sea is not human,
And here is no shore, no intimacy,
Only the start of space, the road to suns.

A Grain of Rice

Such majestic rhythms, such tiny disturbances.
The rain of the monsoon falls, an inescapable treasure,
    hundreds of millions live
Only because of the certainty of this season,
    The turn of the wind.

The frame of our human house rests on the motion
Of earth and of moon, the rise of continents,
Invasion of deserts, erosion of hills,
    The capping of ice.

Today, while Europe tilted, drying the Baltic,
I read of a battle between brothers in anguish,
    A flag moved a mile.

And today, from a curled leaf cocoon, in the course of its
    rhythm,
I saw the break of a shell, the creation
Of a great Asian moth, radiant, fragile,
Incapable of not being born, and trembling
    To live its brief moment.

Religions build walls round our love, and science
Is equal of error and truth. Yet always we find
Such ordered purpose in cell and in galaxy,
So great a glory in life-thrust and mind-range,
Such widening frontiers to draw out our longings,
    We grow to one world through
    Enlargement of wonder.

Conflict

When I see the falling bombs
Then I see defended homes.
Men above and men below
Die to save the good they know.

Through the wrong the bullets prove
Shows the bravery of love.
Pro and con have single stem
Half a truth dividing them.

Between the dagger and the breast
The bond is stronger than the beast.
Prison, ghetto, flag and gun
Mark the craving for the One.

Persecution's cruel mouth
Shows a twisted love of truth.
Deeper than the rack and rope
Lies the double human hope.

My good, your good, good we seek
Though we turn no other cheek.
He who slays and he who's slain
Like in purpose, like in pain.

Who shall bend to single plan
The narrow sacrifice of man?
Find the central human urge
To make a thousand roads converge?

Old Song

far voices
and fretting leaves

this music the
hillside gives

but in the deep
Laurentian river
an elemental song
for ever

a quiet calling
of no mind
out of long aeons
when dust was blind
and ice hid sound

only a moving
with no note
granite lips
a stone throat

Caring

Caring is loving, motionless,
An interval of more and less
Between the stress and the distress.

After the present falls the past,
After the festival, the fast.
Always the deepest is the last.

This is the circle we must trace,
Not spiralled outward, but a space
Returning to its starting place.

Centre of all we mourn and bless,
Centre of calm beyond excess,
Who cares for caring, has caress.

F. R. SCOTT

Bonne Entente

The advantages of living with two cultures
Strike one at every turn,
Especially when one finds a notice in an office building:
'This elevator will not run on Ascension Day';
Or reads in the *Montreal Star:*
'Tomorrow being the Feast of the Immaculate Conception,
There will be no collection of garbage in the city';
Or sees on the restaurant menu the bilingual dish:

DEEP APPLE PIE
TARTE AUX POMMES PROFONDES

Calamity

A laundry truck
Rolled down the hill
And crashed into my maple tree.
It was a truly North American calamity.
Three cans of beer fell out
(Which in itself was revealing)
And a jumble of skirts and shirts
Spilled onto the ploughed grass.
Dogs barked, and the children
Sprouted like dandelions on my lawn.
Normally we do not speak to one another on this avenue,
But the excitement made us suddenly neighbours.
People exchanged remarks
Who had never been introduced
And for a while we were quite human.
Then the policeman came –
Sedately, for this was Westmount –
And carefully took down all names and numbers.
The towing truck soon followed,
Order was restored.
The starch came raining down.

ROBERT FINCH

1900–

Scroll-section

You who practise the four elegant occupations
tea music calligraphy and checkers
follow me over the snow in search of plum blossom.

Leave kingdom breakers
to juggle nations,
and care's broad
cloud
to the white hare that with mortar and pestle
sits in the moon by the cassia tree,
leave your lacquer trestle
of puppets, your aviary
of pets in petrified wood,
your malachite lion with its ball of brocade,
your clique to scribble the past
on dust,
and with no inlaid saddle,
no jewelled bridle,
follow me over the snow in search of plum blossom.

The leaping salmon rainbows the cataracts,
the dragon in chase of a pearl skips space
and the phoenix, alighting, first selects a place
to arrange its tail. Emulate in a degree these agreeable acts.

Silent though peach and plum
a path is trod to them.
Every rustic talent
till seen is silent.
Even the hollow bamboo
has leaves that droop.

Come back over the snow,
set up
wrist-rests, paint in ink
mountains trees creepers clouds
gorges rivers cascades
the brink
of wind, monasteries in mist,
beauties that have no best,
that through your purpose a longing be learned, earned,
the seal of your mind borrowed and not returned.

Jardin de la Chapelle Expiatoire

Expiatory chapel, chains
Of iron and ivy bind the lanes
Below the lightning-rodded dome
That spikes the sun upon your tomb

Where nurses, children, lovers, fools
And wise, and birds, forget their rôles
Watching time guillotine the heads
Of lilies in the lily beds,

While tears from chestnut candles drop
A wreath of wax, and in the shop
Hard by the marchand de couronnes
Retrieves them in a porcelain one.

Newspapers crackle and hoops roll.
The bench unfurls its slatted scroll
To let a Latin lover's arm
Perturb the Saxon sense of form.

Je t'aimerai toujours! – Toujours? –
Toujours, voilà ce qu'est l'amour.
The obedient clock across the park
Marks time all day to that remark.

Trop radical? Monsieur! Je dis . . .
Peut-êtr' que non, peut-êtr' que oui.
The fate of France goes balancing
With pince-nez on a shaken string.

Faut broder tout autour, serré,
Comm' ça ça fait plus distingué.
The mould of fashion is reset
While Louis romps with Antoinette.

Veux-tu te taire! Viens ici!
M'entends-tu? Tu seras puni!
And shaded by historic woes
A mother mops her infant's nose.

Train Window

The dark green truck on the cement platform
is explicit as a paradigm.
Its wheels are four black cast-iron starfish.
Its body, a massive tray of planking,
ends in two close-set dark green uprights
crossed with three straight cross-pieces, one
looped with a white spiral of hose.

The truck holds eleven cakes of ice,
each cake a different size and shape.
Some look as though a weight had hit them.
One, solid glass, has a core of sugar.
They lean, a transitory Icehenge,
in a moor of imitation snow
from the hatchet's bright wet-sided steel.

Five galvanized pails, mottled, as if
of stiffened frosted caracul, three
with crescent lids and elbowed spouts,
loom in the ice, their half-hoop handles

linking that frozen elocution
to the running chalk-talk of powder-red
box-cars beyond, while our train waits here.

Alone

Carry your grief alone,
No other wants it,
Each man has his own,
A fool flaunts it.

Alone, but not unique:
Bubble to bubble
Is not more like
Than trouble to trouble.

Alone, but light in the end,
For time shall whittle
It like the word of a friend
And the body's fettle.

Alone, to the end, and through
To join the solaced,
The steady journey due
To grief's ballast.

The Statue

A small boy has thrown a stone at a statue,
And a man who threatened has told a policeman so.
Down the pathway they rustle in a row,
The boy, the man, the policeman. If you watch you

Will see the alley of trees join in the chase
And the flower-beds stiffly make after the boy,
The fountains brandish their cudgels in his way
And the sky drop a blue netting in his face.

Only the statue unmoved in its moving stillness
Holds the park as before the deed was done
On a stone axis round which the trio whirls.

Stone that endured the chisel's cutting chillness
Is tolerant of the stone at its foot of stone
And the pigeon sitting awry on its carved curls.

L. A. MacKAY

1901–

Admonition for Spring

Look away now from the high lonesome hills
So hard on the hard sky since the swift shower;
See where among the restless daffodils
The hyacinth sets his melancholy tower.

Draw in your heart from vain adventurings;
Float slowly, swimmer, slowly drawing breath.
See, in this wild green foam of growing things
The heavy hyacinth remembering death.

From *Erotica Antiqua*

Propertian

Time-worn, the soldier lays aside the steel,
Time-worn, the patient ox will plough no more,
The swiftest hound will doze, the sturdiest keel
Crumble to rest upon an empty shore;
The gods grow old, and weary of belief.
Only my love lives on, only my grief.

Only my grief lives on, which is my love.
Only my joy, which is my only sorrow,
Lives on; and vulture-like, the ruffling dove
Gropes in his vitals. Never shall any morrow
Bring the huge archer with the murderous bow,
Nor Elbruz cool his veins with all its snow.

'Now there is nothing left'

Now there is nothing left of all our sorrow,
Or only this: to know that sorrow dwindles,

And broken hearts may take their place tomorrow
With love, in the routine of minor swindles.

Doubtless we still shall find that we are able
To call a ghost up, with a little trying,
And learn, like many more, that life's a cable
Twisted of tedious, small, unfinished dyings.

'Look, I have thrown all right'

Look, I have thrown all right to love you into the ditch
If there are such rights – thrown it into the public road
In the miry spots, and jumped and stamped on it, yelling as loud
As my bursting lungs could scream, to gather a crowd
That would look on, and jeer, while I laid the switch
On the trembling ribs of the love that was so proud
A little while ago, thought himself so rich,
So masterly – look at him shivering without now a stitch! –
Though on my own nakedness most the lashes showed.

I have thrown all right to love you into the mire.
I tell you my love would defile you now by its touch.
It was scorched, discoloured, deformed, besmirched by the fire,
The tinsel gilt withered up to a dirty smutch;
And out of the ashes it was not a phoenix flew,
But a grimy soot-fouled worm crept out from the pyre
Lifting a mute and horrible face still towards you.

A. J. M. SMITH

1902–

On Knowing Nothing

Others have seen men die
Or heard a woman scream
One last word *Never*!
How do I know the horror
That breaks the dream,
Hateful yet clung to
As the image hugs the mirror
With such a silver shiver
As chills and almost kills?

I know: but how or why
Out of this savory fatness I
Should suck the sharp surmise
That strangles dying eyes
I do not know. What have I done
To bring the Angel round my head
That I can smell his pinion
(Bond or wing?)
Whom I must hate and love?

The surgeon's jab, a woman's thigh
Give blank surcease
For short or long.
I cannot let the hollow
Interval alone,
But pick it like a scab
To probe the wound within –
As deep, as nothing, as the grave.

News of the Phoenix

They say the Phoenix is dying, some say dead.
Dead without issue is what one message said,
But that has been suppressed, officially denied.

I think myself the man who sent it lied.
In any case, I'm told, he has been shot,
As a precautionary measure, whether he did or not.

Ode: On the Death of William Butler Yeats

An old thorn tree in a stony place
Where the mountain stream has run dry,
Torn in the black wind under the race
Of the icicle-sharp kaleidoscopic white sky,
   Bursts into sudden flower.

Under the central dome of winter and night
A wild swan spreads his fanatic wing.
Ancestralled energy of blood and power
Beats in his sinewy breast. And now the ravening
Soul, fulfilled, his first-last hour
   Upon him, chooses to exult.

Over the edge of shivering Europe,
Over the chalk front of Kent, over Eire,
Dwarfing the crawling waves' amoral savagery,
Daring the hiding clouds' rhetorical tumult,
   The white swan plummets the mountain top.

The stream has suddenly pushed the papery leaves!
It digs a rustling channel of clear water
On the scarred flank of Ben Bulben.
The twisted tree is incandescent with flowers.

The swan leaps singing into the cold air:
This is a glory not for an hour:
Over the Galway shore
The white bird is flying
Forever, and crying
To the tumultuous throng
Of the sky his cold and passionate song.

The Plot against Proteus

This is a theme for muted coronets
To dangle from debilitated heads
Of navigation, kings, or riverbeds
That rot or rise what time the seamew sets
Her course by stars among the smoky tides
Entangled. Old saltencrusted Proteus treads
Once more the watery shore that water weds
While rocking fathom bell rings round and rides.

Now when the blind king of the water thinks
The sharp hail of the salt out of his eyes
To abdicate, run thou, O Prince, and fall
Upon him. This cracked walrus skin that stinks
Of the rank sweat of a mermaid's thighs
Cast off, and nab him; when you have him, call.

The Archer

Bend back thy bow, O Archer, till the string
Is level with thine ear, thy body taut,
Its nature art, thyself thy statue wrought
Of marble blood, thy weapon the poised wing
Of coiled and aquiline Fate. Then, loosening, fling
The hissing arrow like a burning thought
Into the empty sky that smokes as the hot
Shaft plunges to the bullseye's quenching ring.

So for a moment, motionless, serene,
Fixed between time and time, I aim and wait;
Nothing remains for breath now but to waive
His prior claim and let the barb fly clean
Into the heart of what I know and hate –
That central black, the ringed and targeted grave.

Far West

Among the cigarettes and the peppermint creams
Came the flowers of fingers, luxurious and bland,
Incredibly blossoming in the little breast.
And in the Far West
The tremendous cowboys in goatskin pants
Shot up the town of her ignorant wish.

In the gun flash she saw the long light shake
Across the lake, repeating that poem
At Finsbury Park.
But the echo was drowned in the roll of the trams –
Anyway, who would have heard? Not a soul.
Not one noble and toxic like Buffalo Bill.

In the holy name *bang! bang!* the flowers came
With the marvellous touch of fingers
Gentler than the fuzzy goats
Moving up and down up and down as if in ecstasy
As the cowboys rode their skintight stallions
Over the barbarous hills of California.

The Wisdom of Old Jelly Roll

How all men wrongly death to dignify
Conspire, I tell. Parson, poetaster, pimp,
Each acts or acquiesces. They prettify,

Dress up, deodorise, embellish, primp,
And make a show of Nothing. Ah, but met-
aphysics laughs: she touches, tastes, and smells
– Hence knows – the diamond holes that make a net.
Silence resettled testifies to bells.
'Nothing' depends on 'Thing', which is or was:
So death makes life or makes life's worth, a worth
Beyond all highfalutin' woes or shows
To publish and confess. 'Cry at the birth,
Rejoice at the death,' old Jelly Roll said,
Being on whiskey, ragtime, chicken, and the scriptures fed.

The Sorcerer

There is a sorcerer in Lachine
Who for a small fee will put a spell
On my beloved, who has sea-green
Eyes, and on my doting self as well.

He will transform us, if we like, to goldfish:
We shall swim in a crystal bowl,
And the bright water will go swish
Over our naked bodies; we shall have no soul.

In the morning the syrupy sunshine
Will dance on our tails and fins.
I shall have her then all for mine,
And Father Lebeau will hear no more of her sins.

Come along, good sir, change us into goldfish.
I would put away intellect and lust,
Be but a red gleam in a crystal dish,
But kin of the trembling ocean, not of the dust.

ROY DANIELLS

1902–

From *Deeper into the Forest*

I never swung a staff and deep, oh deep
I've buried all my books that no leaf turn
Under the turning autumn leaves that sleep
In late sun or in blazes and blue smoke burn.

I never met Miranda; I would scorn
To look in when she's found and wound her man
And says she's very lucky to be born. –
I'm going berry-picking, with Caliban.

My nerves are frayed; my hair is come uncurled;
But Caliban has a snack for two all packed.
We bid a glad good-bye to the brave new world;
We won't be back to see the final act.

Farewell the ship, and so long to the crew!
Good-bye to playwrights, and good-bye to you!

Noah

They gathered around and told him not to do it,
They formed a committee and tried to take control,
They cancelled his building permit and they stole
His plans. I sometimes wonder he got through it.
He told them wrath was coming, they would rue it,
He begged them to believe the tides would roll,
He offered them passage to his destined goal,
A new world. They were finished and he knew it.
All to no end.
 And then the rain began.

A spatter at first that barely wet the soil,
Then showers, quick rivulets lacing the town,
Then deluge universal. The old man
Arthritic from his years of scorn and toil
Leaned from the admiral's walk and watched them drown.

R. G. EVERSON

1903–

Child with Shell

We two lying on sand –
dozens of wrestling lovers twined
in never-ending August love –
while a child scrapes scrapes a shell,
the inside,
to get the deep watery colour off.

Not turned back by Quebec citadel
or mountains pressing down from the land,
the tide
pushes far inland here towards Trois-Rivières.

The child scrapes scrapes away
at the shell –
always the same swirling colour shown;
it won't come off.
A waste of time, child. It's in the bone,
like tides and love.

When I'm Going Well

When I'm going well
as now at Westmount Glen and CPR
in wet October dusk, the winds
taste firecrackery. Loud sparks
jump up laughing like a Breughel bride.
Crayoned in phosphorus, the station agent
vibrates. He's electrocuted.

When I'm electrocuted
weather doesn't matter: wet

dusk of October flashes fire well
like Summer moon, March mud.
I dance on tiptoe mind along the platform
shaking laughter's outstretched hands
that shock me like a Winter lightswitch.

When I'm a Winter lightswitch
I pick allusions off the railway tracks.
Climbing a signal standard, I wave my hat.
A girl walking by along the platform
explodes the whole Glen area.

Rogue Pearunners

We drove – our autoload gang – through the growing season,
a stroll of beaters spread along seed farms,
uprooting rogue pearunners and wild flowers
to nourish the chosen seed.

I felt religious
in a priest-walk meadow of green-leather peastrings
that held earth down safely. Thousands of acres
in the townships of Rama, Mara and Thora
blurred back under my mind.

I am dismayed in anger at rogue pearunners
and strange flowering weeds.
I strangle all peculiar growing things,
hating them worse than abstract artistry.

I suffer an apprehension of petals,
lest the mind open
with intuitions and imaginings.

EARLE BIRNEY

1904–

Pacific Door

Through or over the deathless feud
of the cobra sea and the mongoose wind
you must fare to reach us
Through hiss and throttle come
by a limbo of motion humbled
under cliffs of cloud
and over the shark's blue home.
Across the undulations of this slate
long pain and sweating courage chalked
such names as glimmer yet
Drake's crewmen scribbled here their paradise
and dying Bering lost in fog
turned north to mark us off from Asia still
Here cool Cook traced in sudden blood his final bay
and scurvied traders trailed the wakes of yesterday
until the otter rocks were bare
and all the tribal feathers plucked
Here Spaniards and Vancouver's boatmen scrawled
the problem that is ours and yours
that there is no clear Strait of Anian
to lead us easy back to Europe
that men are isled in ocean or in ice
and only joined by long endeavour to be joined
Come then on the waves of desire that well forever
and think no more than you must
of the simple unhuman truth of this emptiness
that down deep below the lowest pulsing of primal cell
tar-dark and still
lie the bleak and forever capacious tombs of the sea

EARLE BIRNEY

This Page My Pigeon

This page is my pigeon sailing
out of the blasted Now to you
my greenest past   my rivered future
See   round his leg snug   love's cylinder

come from this world of wild undoing
from all this quarrel of iron and growth
Weaving by snake-pit of ack-ack and robot's
roar-horror   up past the beautiful brutal

bombers floating like flakes of mica
leaps my faithful feathered one   soars
through the haired and dirty clouds of war
cleaving cleanly the selfcentred sky

Under apathetic suns and over
the pointless ocean he arrows   off
to the one unlosable loft
What does he say for me   what brings my homer?

Says that your voice still waters my memory
your eyes are leads to the wide light
that will be   Swears you are part of the rightness
of hills   the saneness of music and hemlocks

Says the giraffish dockweed   loneliness
was lopped away long ago   burned in your vaulting fire
when first you gardened me   Now this gyring
windstorm of absence whirls ashes up only

Windseed is barren   takes no truehold
in heart tendrilled tight with existence of you

EARLE BIRNEY

Bushed

He invented a rainbow but lightning struck it
shattered it into the lake-lap of a mountain
so big his mind slowed when he looked at it

Yet he built a shack on the shore
learned to roast porcupine belly and
wore the quills on his hatband

At first he was out with the dawn
whether it yellowed bright as wood-columbine
or was only a fuzzed moth in a flannel of storm
But he found the mountain was clearly alive
sent messages whizzing down every hot morning
boomed proclamations at noon and spread out
a white guard of goat
before falling asleep on its feet at sundown

When he tried his eyes on the lake   ospreys
would fall like valkyries
choosing the cut-throat
He took then to waiting
till the night smoke rose from the boil of the sunset

But the moon carved unknown totems
out of the lakeshore
owls in the beardusky woods derided him
moosehorned cedars circled his swamps and tossed
their antlers up to the stars
Then he knew   though the mountain slept   the winds
were shaping its peak to an arrowhead
poised

But by now he could only
bar himself in and wait
for the great flint to come singing into his heart

EARLE BIRNEY

Slug in Woods

For eyes he waves greentipped
taut horns of slime   They dipped
hours back   across a reef
a salmonberry leaf
Then strained to grope past fin
of spruce   Now eyes suck in
as through the hemlock butts
of his day's ledge there cuts
a vixen chipmunk   Stilled
is he – green mucus chilled
or blotched and soapy stone
pinguid in moss   alone
Hours on   he will resume
his silver scrawl   illume
his palimpsest   emboss
his diver's line across
that waving green illim-
itable seafloor   Slim
young jay his sudden shark
the wrecks he skirts are dark
and fungussed firlogs   whom
spirea sprays emplume
encoral   Dew his shell
while mounting boles foretell
of isles in dappled air
fathoms above his care
Azygous muted life
himself his viscid wife
foodward he noses cold beneath his sea
So spends a summer's jasper century

Mappemounde

No not this old   whalehall can whelm us
shiptamed gullgraced   soft to our glidings

Harrows that mere more   which squares our map
See in its north   where scribe has marked *mermen*
shore-sneakers who croon   to the seafarer's girl
next year's gleewords   East and west *nadders*
flamefanged bale-twisters   their breath dries up tears
chars in the breast-hoard   the brave picture-faces
Southward *Cetegrande* that   sly beast who sucks in
with whirlwind also   the wanderer's pledges
That sea is hight Time   it hems all hearts' landtrace
Men say the redeless   reaching its bounds
topple in maelstrom   tread back never
Adread in that mere   we drift to map's end

El Greco: *Espolio*

The carpenter is intent on the pressure of his hand

on the awl   and the trick of pinpointing his strength
through the awl to the wood   which is tough
He has no effort to spare for despoilings
or to worry if he'll be cut in on the dice
His skill is vital to the scene   and the safety of the state
Anyone can perform the indignities   It's his hard arms
and craft that hold the eyes of the convict's women
There is the problem of getting the holes exact
(in the middle of this elbowing crowd)
and deep enough to hold the spikes
after they've sunk through those bared feet
and inadequate wrists he knows are waiting behind him

He doesn't sense perhaps that one of the hands
is held in a curious gesture over him –
giving   or asking   forgiveness? –
but he'd scarcely take time to be puzzled by poses
Criminals come in all sorts   as anyone knows who makes
crosses
are as mad or sane as those who decide on their killings

Our one at least has been quiet so far
though they say he has talked himself into this trouble
a carpenter's son who got notions of preaching

Well heres a carpenter's son who'll have carpenter sons,
God willing   and build what's wanted   temples or tables
mangers or crosses   and shape them decently
working alone in that firm and profound abstraction
which blots out the bawling of rag-snatchers
To construct with hands   knee-weight   braced thigh
keeps the back turned from death

But it's too late now for the other carpenter's boy
to return to this peace before the nails are hammered

Irapuato

For reasons any
brigadier
could tell
this is a favourite nook for
massacre
Toltex by Mixtex Mixtex by Aztex
Aztex by Spanishtex Spanishtex by
Mexitex by Mexitex by Mexitex by Texaco

So any farmer can see how the strawberries
are the biggest and reddest
in the whole damn continent

but why
when arranged under
the market flies

do they look like small clotting hearts?

ALFRED G. BAILEY

1905–

Shrouds and Away

The great fear is expected to flash
and curl the toenails of the curly ape,
too self-domesticated yet to scream
and fold his arms up in a sliding down,
his punctured skull as by a forty-five
away in the mesquite, away back
in the atomic saloons of the cowboy frontier,
not alone but replete with buckskin death.
Saddled was no way to escape, as even
Dodge City, or Tombstone, or Bisbee
could grow in a red fester
                over the chest of the earth
from the heart outwards and into the
                fronded parts,
leaving them listless, and tested without meaning
or direction or hate. For to fare upwards
in a new life of the heart, keeping the
head turned lifeward, it was essential
to unloop the soul on a mountain peak
and stock up on new (if such could be found)
lodes of a kind of ore we could not assay
                from prior experience,
(to turn back was certain death in the dark)
but one demanding a naked advance into a
                land of terror and flowering saguaro
because even the greatest philosophers have
sides that droop and lie about their
loins and mock the lean
and ever-recurrent splendour of the eaglet.

LEO KENNEDY

1907–

Words for a Resurrection

Each pale Christ stirring underground
Splits the brown casket of its root,
Wherefrom the rousing soil upthrusts
A narrow, pointed shoot,

And bones long quiet under frost
Rejoice as bells precipitate
The loud, ecstatic sundering,
The hour inviolate.

This Man of April walks again –
Such marvel does the time allow –
With laughter in His blessèd bones,
And lilies on His brow.

Mole Talk

The weasel and the wren consort,
  Beneath one coverlet,
Upon the whittled bones of each
  Docility is set;
Strange fellows for a common bed,
  The rodent and the bird
Lip-deep in sand and gravel, lie
  Without a grudging word.
No shuddering disports the worm,
  Too wise are they, and proud,
To lift a stiffened limb, or pluck
  The seaming of a shroud.

JOHN GLASSCO

1909–

Quebec Farmhouse

Admire the face of plastered stone,
The roof descending like a song
Over the washed and anointed walls,
Over the house that hugs the earth
Like a feudal souvenir: oh see
The sweet submissive fortress of itself
That the landscape owns!

And inside is the night, the airless dark
Of the race so conquered it has made
Perpetual conquest of itself,
Upon desertion's ruin piling
The inward desert of surrender,
Drawing in all its powers, puffing its soul,
Raising its arms to God.

This is the closed, enclosing house
That set its flinty face against
The rebel children dowered with speech
To break it open, to make it live
And flower in the cathedral beauty
Of a pure heaven of Canadian blue –
The larks so maimed

They still must hark and hurry back
To the paradisal place of gray,
The clash of keys, the click of beads,
The sisters walking leglessly,
While under the wealth and weight of stone
All the bright demons of forbidden joy
Shriek on, year after year.

JOHN GLASSCO

Utrillo's World

I

He sat above it, watching it recede,
A world of love resolved to empty spaces,
Streets without figures, figures without faces,
Desolate by choice and negative from need.
But the hoardings weep, the shutters burn and bleed;
Colours of crucifixion, dying graces,
Spatter and cling upon these sorrowful places.
– Where is the loved one? Where do the streets lead?

There is no loved one. Perfect fear
Has cast out love. And the streets go on forever
To blest annihilation, silently ascend
To their own assumption of bright points in air . . .
It is the world that counts, the endless fever,
And suffering that is its own and only end.

II

Anguished these sombre houses, still, resigned.
Suffering has found no better face than wood
For its own portrait: tears are not so good
As the last reticence of being blind.
Grief without voice, mourning without mind,
I find your silence in this neighbourhood;
These hideous places ransom with their blood
The shame and self-loathing of mankind.

They are also masks that misery has put on
Over the faces and the festivals:
Madness and fear must have a place to hide,
And murder a secret room to call its own.
We know they are prisons also, the thin walls
Between us and what cowers and shakes inside.

JOHN GLASSCO

Brummell at Calais

A foolish useless man who had done nothing
All his life long but keep himself clean,
Locked in the glittering armour of a pose
Made up of impudence, chastity and reserve –
How does his memory still survive his world?

The portraits show us only a tilted nose,
Lips full blown, a cravat and curly wig,
And a pair of posturing eyes,
Infinitely vulnerable, deeply innocent,
Their malice harmless as a child's:

And he has returned to childhood now, his stature
That of the Butterfly whose *Funeral*
He sang (his only song) for one of his
Dear duchesses, Frances or Georgiana,
In the intolerable metre of Tom Moore –

To a childhood of sweet biscuits and curaçao;
Hair-oil and tweezers make him forget his debts,
The angle of his hat remains the same,
His little boots pick their way over the cobblestones,
But where is he going as well as going mad?

Nowhere: his glory is already upon him,
The fading Regency man who will leave behind
More than the ankle-buttoning pantaloon!
For see, even now in the long implacable twilight,
The triumph of his veritable art,

An art of being, nothing but being, the grace
Of perfect self-assertion based on nothing,
As in our vanity's cause against the void
He strikes his elegant blow, the solemn report of those
Who have done nothing and will never die.

A. M. KLEIN

1909–

Heirloom

My father bequeathed me no wide estates;
No keys and ledgers were my heritage;
Only some holy books with *yahrzeit* dates
Writ mournfully upon a blank front page –

Books of the Baal Shem Tov, and of his wonders;
Pamphlets upon the devil and his crew;
Prayers against road demons, witches, thunders;
And sundry other tomes for a good Jew.

Beautiful: though no pictures on them, save
The scorpion crawling on a printed track;
The Virgin floating on a scriptural wave,
Square letters twinkling in the Zodiac.

The snuff left on this page, now brown and old,
The tallow stains of midnight liturgy –
These are my coat of arms, and these unfold
My noble lineage, my proud ancestry!

And my tears, too, have stained this heirloomed ground,
When reading in these treatises some weird
Miracle, I turned a leaf and found
A white hair fallen from my father's beard.

The Still Small Voice

The candles splutter; and the kettle hums;
The heirloomed clock enumerates the tribes,
Upon the wine-stained table-cloth lie crumbs
Of matzoh whose wide scattering describes

Jews driven in far lands upon this earth.
The kettle hums; the candles splutter; and
Winds whispering from shutters tell re-birth
Of beauty rising in an eastern land,
Of paschal sheep driven in cloudy droves;
Of almond-blossoms colouring the breeze;
Of vineyards upon verdant terraces;
Of golden globes in orient orange-groves.
And those assembled at the table dream
Of small schemes that an April wind doth scheme,
And cry from out the sleep assailing them:
Jerusalem, next year! Next year, Jerusalem!

From *The Psalter of Avram Haktani*

PSALM VI

A psalm of Abraham, concerning that which
he beheld upon the heavenly scarp:

I

And on that day, upon the heavenly scarp,
The hosannahs ceased, the hallelujahs died,
And music trembled on the silenced harp.
An angel, doffing his seraphic pride,
Wept; and his tears so bitter were, and sharp,
That where they fell, the blossoms shrivelled and died.

II

Another with such voice intoned his psalm
It sang forth blasphemy against the Lord.
Oh, that was a very imp in angeldom,
Who, thinking evil, said no evil word –
But only pointed, at each *Te Deum*
Down to the earth, and its abhorrèd horde.

III

The Lord looked down, and saw the cattle-cars:
Men ululating to a frozen land.
He saw a man tear at his flogged scars,
And saw a babe look for its blown-off hand.
Scholars, he saw, sniffing their bottled wars,
And doctors who had geniuses unmanned.

IV

The gentle violinist whose fingers played
Such godly music, washing a pavement, with lye,
He saw. He heard the priest who called His aid.
He heard the agnostic's undirected cry.
Unto Him came the odor Hunger made,
And the odor of blood before it is quite dry.

V

The angel who wept looked into the eyes of God.
The angel who sang ceased pointing to the earth.
A little cherub, now glimpsing God's work flaw'd,
Went mad, and flapped his wings in crazy mirth.
And the good Lord said nothing, but with a nod
Summoned the angels of Sodom down to earth.

PSALM XII

To the chief musician, who played
for the dancers:

These were the ones who thanked their God
With dancing jubilant shins:
The beggar, who for figleaf pride
Sold shoelaces and pins;
The blindman for his brotherly dog;
The cripple for his chair;
The mauled one for the blessed gasp
Of the cone of sweet kind air.

I did not see this dance, but men
Have praised its grace; yet I
Still cannot fathom how they danced,
Or why.

The Rocking Chair

It seconds the crickets of the province. Heard
in the clean lamplit farmhouses of Quebec, –
wooden, – it is no less a national bird;
and rivals, in its cage, the mere stuttering clock.
To its time, the evenings are rolled away;
and in its peace the pensive mother knits
contentment to be worn by her family,
grown-up, but still cradled by the chair in which she sits.

It is also the old man's pet, pair to his pipe,
the two aids of his arithmetic and plans,
plans rocking and puffing into market-shape;
and it is the toddler's game and dangerous dance.
Moved to the verandah, on summer Sundays, it is,
among the hanging plants, the girls, the boy-friends,
sabbatical and clumsy, like the white haloes
dangling above the blue serge suits of the young men.

It has a personality of its own;
is a character (like that old drunk Lacoste,
exhaling amber, and toppling on his pins);
it is alive; individual; and no less
an identity than those about it. And
it is tradition. Centuries have been flicked
from its arcs, alternatively flicked and pinned.
It rolls with the gait of St Malo. It is act

and symbol, symbol of this static folk
which moves in segments, and returns to base, –
a sunken pendulum: *invoke, revoke;*

loosed yon, leashed hither, motion on no space.
O, like some Anjou ballad, all refrain,
which turns about its longing, and seems to move
to make a pleasure out of repeated pain,
its music moves, as if always back to a first love.

Bread

Creation's crust and crumb, breaking of bread,
Seedstaff and wheatwand of all miracles,
By your white fiat, at the feast-times said,
World moves, and is revived the shrouded pulse!
Rising, as daily rises the quickening east,
O kneading of knowledge, leaven of happiness,
History yearns upon your yearning yeast!
No house is home without your wifeliness.

No city stands up from its rock-bound knees
Without your rustic aid. None are elect
Save you be common. All philosophies
Betray them with your yokel dialect.

O black-bread hemisphere, oblong of rye,
Crescent and circle of the seeded bun,
All art is builded on your geometry,
All science explosive from your captured sun.

Bakers most priestly, in your robes of flour,
White Levites at your altar'd ovens, bind,
Bind me forever in your ritual, your
Worship and prayer, me, and all mankind!

MALCOLM LOWRY

1909–57

'Cain shall not slay Abel today on our good ground'

Cain shall not slay Abel today on our good ground,
Nor Adam stagger on our shrouded moon,
Nor Ishmael lie stiff in 28th Street,
With a New Bedford harpoon in his brain,
His right lung in a Hoboken garboon.
For this is the long day when the lost are found,
And those, parted by tragedy, meet
With spring-sweet joy. And those who longest should have met
Are safe in each other's arms not too late.
Today the forsaken one of the fold is brought home,
And the great cold, in the street of the vulture, are warm,
The numbed albatross is sheltered from the storm,
The tortured shall no longer know alarm
For all in wilderness are free from harm:
Age dreaming on youth, youth dreaming on age, shall not be found,
While good Loki chases dragons underground.
Life hears our prayer for the lonely trimmer on watch,
Or shuddering, at one bell, on the wet hatch,
At evening, for the floating sailor by the far coast,
The impaled soldier in the shell-hole or the hail,
The crew of the doomed barque sweeping into the sunset
With black sails; for mothers in anguish and unrest
And each of all the oppressed, a compassionate ghost
Will recommend the Pentecost.
Ah, poets of God's mercy, harbingers of the gale,
Now I say the lamb is brought home, and Gogol
Wraps a warm overcoat about him. . . .
Our city of dreadful night will blossom into a sea-morning!
Only bear with us, bear with my song,
For at dawn is the reckoning and the last night is long.

Lupus in Fabula

Those animals that follow us in dream,
And mean I know not what! But what of those
That hunt us, snuff, stalk us out in life, close
In upon it, belly-down, haunt our scheme
Of building, with shapes of delirium,
Symbols of death, heraldic, and shadows
Glowering? – Just before we left Tlampam
Our cats lay quivering under the maguey;
A meaning had slunk, and now died, with them.
The boy slung them half stiff down the ravine,
Which now we entered, and whose name is hell.
But still our last night had its animal:
The puppy, in the cabaret, obscene,
Looping-the-loop, and dirtying the floor,
And fastening itself to that horror
Of our last night: and the very last day
While I sat bowed, frozen over mescal,
They dragged two shrieking fawns through the hotel
And slit their throats, behind the barroom door....

DOROTHY LIVESAY

1909–

From *The Colour of God's Face*

1. *The Land*

I

Implacable woman
the land reclines: dusty deaf
heart of stillness   mummified stillness
black

Sun rages   month on month
and men light fires   make trees totter
for fertile ash

But suddenly in November
a bird's voice fountains
thunder rants
rains tantrum
demanding   demanding

In a green swing upwards
the soil yields –
                    the land is dancing!

II

The still trees in late afternoon
are nameless elements
like elms they soar
like mushrooms wreathe the sky
At night they burst out suddenly
and fructify
with ripe moon-silvered fruit,
parade in columns
toward blue stars:

until the loud cicada shrills
telling the world their names.

2. *The People*

Village

Nameless, the village
the clay huts, the shorn grass roof
brown to the ground
nameless
the woman huddled outside beside a pale flame
and the child, bringing stools to sit upon
is nameless, boy or girl

They do not love this place, or name it
they are too much of it:
they smell of grass, of leaves,
of the pitiless dust
they rise up with the rain
and die with it

Between the land and themselves
they feel no difference
loving the earth no more than a man loves his own hand
Use it, and live
or cut it off, and die.

Wedding

At the periphery and fringe
of villages where drumming swings
the hand that does the drumming
moves the world
meets sun halfway
and hauls him over the rim

The hand that does the drumming
drums man home
to womb and woman
beats that rhythm
on black curving thighs
thrusts love upward

The Leader

I

But the Copperbelt night is a snake
strangling the drums
squeezing the air
from throats, from lungs;
under its arching coils
a child's cry shrills
in the beerhall's roar
a cauldron boils.

The Copperbelt day is saved
by a strike of thunder
the man on the anthill
crying out 'Kwatcha!'
Wilder than rain pelt
or the beat of sunlight
children shout freedom
waving green branches

II

Heaven lets down a rope
whereon I swing
the clapper of a bell
on sounding sky

And all below
they cluster with uplifted faces
black on white
and sway like flowers
to my wild clanging

Whether sun burns me
or moon rivets with steely eye
I shall ring on
till flowers are black mouths
and the stones bleed my song.

Republic of Zambia

RALPH GUSTAFSON

1909–

Carta Canadensis

The land starts *dentelle*, indented,
With tidemark of hills, broadens
Into dark green canting
Over rock eternal with loneliness,
Northwestward tilting from granite
The ochre lakes. This
Is the great Shield clamped
On the place of love. Only
At the tide and inland littoral
Is there literal love. Wharves
Wash on the waves of wheat
Husky with summer luck,
In autumn harvested on the plains.
Fish and wheat, the promise,
Christ and bread,
Brought to the tables of
An iron land.
Backward
Up against the possible
East, the broken mountains
Of magnificence
Sheering the plainsoil northward
Out of sight, roses
Lean, provincial, burning
In their plot.

Legend

Whoever is washed ashore at that place –
Many come there but thrust by so fierce a sun
The great cliffs cast no shadow, plunge a passage

Inland where foliage and whistling paradise-birds
Offer comfort – whoever has got up,
Standing, certainty under his adjusting heels
And height tugged by the tide, ocean rinsing
From flank and belly, ravelling loins with wet,
Whoever has stayed, solitary in those tropics,
The caverns of his chest asking acres,
he,
Doomed in that landscape but among magnificence,
By shell and seafoam tampered with, his senses
As though by her of Aeaea used, exquisite –
He, that salt upon his time's tongue,
Knows, standing the margin ocean and sand,
Ilium toppled thunder his ears, what's left
Of Helen naked drag between his toes.

Armorial

I lay down with my love and there was song
Breaking, like the lilies I once saw
Lovely around King Richard, murdered
Most foully and all his grace at Pomfret,
The roses of England stolen; our love
Was like gules emblazoned at Canterbury
Most kingly in windows and leopards
Passant on bars of gold. This
Was our heraldry.

Our love was larks and sprang from meadows
Far from kingdoms, which regal grew
With rod and bloodred weed and rush
Where water ran; this was our love,
The place where she chose, I could not but come,
A field without myth or rhetoric.
She lay down with love and my hand
Was gold with dust of lily. This
Was our province.

There was song in that kingly country
But I saw there, stuck like a porcupine
On Bosworth Field the arrows through him,
That regal and most royal other
Richard, runt and twitch in a ditch,
His hand wristdeep in lily where
Henry Tudor rolled him, the gules
Of England draining on his shirt.
My love wept.

Aspects of Some Forsythia Branches

Waiting for these dry sticks in a vase –
Cut (with deliberate shears taken
From the third drawer down on the left) from the bush
In snow – complicated with leaf
And yellow in the earth elaborated, even
In the wintering sun; as the spiral of a protein
Divides and duplicates the thrust
Of love, the hereditary nose of Caesar,
Alexander's brow and Jennie's
Mole; the aggregation of a galaxy:
So the April science of a bunch
Of sticks cut for an etched glass vase –
Waiting for these to flower in a March
Room – waiting for all this business –
As an act of love, a science of gravel,
A suffering, is this not done
With reliance? One way, dry sticks
Lead to buds, presumably wanted,
To yellow eventually. What trivial aspects
Can be got! We handle love
For small purposes. Yet they serve.
Shrubs are cut for what is believed in.
Somewhere death's in it. Dignity
Is demanded even for the dead.
So we cut branches two

Days ago. Take great precautions.
Go carefully through a door. Stand
Among deathbeds as though among heroes,
Pausing in winter along windy corridors
With the knowledge ahead of us, to wrap our throats.

On this Sea-Floor

The evening falls. The sunset burns
The edge of grass. Where the beach fence
Climbs down, the curlews are done with history.
Sea-tide

On the rocks lifts kelp and is fecund.
The shaped oyster sucks himself in
In sand and the razor-clam zips and is floorless vertical.
Under the ocean

The crab crawls, dragging an entrail.
On this sea-floor there is no disparity.
Conches blown by sea-boys are filled with stomach.
Delicacies void.

Acceptances inhere. Haphazard
The efficient Laughter's driven home.
In salty caverns rests the perfect squid.
Men die.

Shoreward fish affirm the sense
Of humour. On the beach at Viareggio,
Byron turned and was sick, Shelley failing
To burn in the pyre,

The guts salt-soaked – a reasonable
Wetness, yet the legend how
These tidal waters roll upon the world,
A claptrap work.

Oedipus innocent wipes his jelly
Eyes; Job recounts his boils.
Limbless birth exemplifies the banter.
Byron, rather,

Threw up. We use an only insolence,
That gropings should extend to men
And glories wash the steady stars; bring
Down God;

Wrapping up our ocean elegies
In thunderous jests, turning deaf ears
To the hobnob silence of the empty shores;
Try our luck –

Dragging up Jonah with our whale
And fizzling Icarus with our wits.
Hamlet plays his ghost at Elsinore.
The catch is considerable:

Caesar dines and Alexander
Catches cold. Beethoven rages.
From the Parthenon, the Venetian lowers Athena's chariot,
Brings down the house.

The joke's in us – not loud enough
To drown the salted heavens. . . . We have
A like compassion. Lear in his rain, crying
O, O,

And age on the pavement of 14th Street. . . .
The soft-haired prawn is ensconced in his kingdom.
Stars congregate and mark the runnings of
The ebbing tide. . . .

The lighthouse catches the mermaids' bums.
Shells hold sea-thunder.
On the sands, his trident weedy and crown awry,
Old Proteus naps.

ANNE WILKINSON

1910–61

Lens

I

The poet's daily chore
Is my long duty;
To keep and cherish my good lens
For love and war
And wasps about the lilies
And mutiny within.

My woman's eye is weak
And veiled with milk;
My working eye is muscled
With a curious tension,
Stretched and open
As the eyes of children;
Trusting in its vision
Even should it see
The holy holy spirit gambol
Counterheadwise,
Lithe and warm as any animal.

My woman's iris circles
A blind pupil;
The poet's eye is crystal,
Polished to accept the negative,
The contradictions in a proof
And the accidental
Candour of the shadows;
The shutter, oiled and smooth
Clicks on the grace of heroes
Or on some bestial act
When lit with radiance

The afterwords the actors speak
Give depths to violence,
Or if the bull is great
And the matador
And the sword
Itself the metaphor.

II

In my dark room the years
Lie in solution,
Develop film by film.
Slow at first and dim
Their shadows bite
On the fine white pulp of paper.

An early snap of fire
Licking the arms of air
I hold against the light, compare
The details with a prehistoric view
Of land and sea
And cradles of mud that rocked
The wet and sloth of infancy.

A stripe of tiger, curled
And sleeping on the ribs of reason
Prints as clear
As Eve and Adam, pearled
With sweat, staring at an apple core;
And death, in black and white
Or politic in green and Easter film,
Lands on steely points, a dancer
Disciplined to the foolscap stage,
The property of poets
Who command his robes, expose
His moving likeness on the page.

ANNE WILKINSON

'In June and gentle oven'

In June and gentle oven
Summer kingdoms simmer
As they come
And flower and leaf and love
Release
Their sweetest juice.

No wind at all
On the wide green world
Where fields go stroll-
ing by
And in and out
An adder of a stream
Parts the daisies
On a small Ontario farm.

And where, in curve of meadow,
Lovers, touching, lie,
A church of grass stands up
And walls them, holy, in.

Fabulous the insects
Stud the air
Or walk on running water,
Klee-drawn saints
And bright as angels are.

Honeysuckle here
Is more than bees can bear
And time turns pale
And stops to catch its breath
And lovers slip their flesh
And light as pollen
Play on treble water
Till bodies reappear
And a shower of sun
To dry their languor.

Then two in one the lovers lie
And peel the skin of summer
With their teeth
And suck its marrow from a kiss
So charged with grace
The tongue, all knowing
Holds the sap of June
Aloof from seasons, flowing.

A Cautionary Tale

. . . we had sold our death . . . for the sum of £70. 18s. 6d.
and lent our fear . . . on interest of £3. 10s. 0d. per month,
so we did not care about death and we did not fear again.
From *The Palm Wine Drinkard* by Amos Tutuola

She met a lion face to face
As she went walking
Up to her hips in grass
On the wild savannah.
So close they stood they touched
If she put out her thumb
Or he his soft ferocious paw.
She bore no weight of fear,
For only yesterday
She'd leased it to a rich man, poor
In that commodity.
Without her terror she was free
From the alarming smell
That irritates a lion
And makes him lash his tail.
And so he yawned, and stretched
On the long stemmed grasses,
And in the pouring sun
She sat beside his royalty
And sang to him a tale of moon.

Before he rose to go
He opened wide his jaw
And took between his teeth
Her wishing bone, as if to say,
I could, you know.
A rich man had her caution
So she laughed; cool,
In the lion's ear, her pretty breath.
What happened next happens
To every maiden fair
Who lends her fear
But forgets to sell her death:
The lion ate her up, and down
To the smallest crumb.
Lord have mercy upon
Her sweet white bones. Amen.

From *Nature Be Damned*

I took my watch beside the rose;
I saw the worm move in;
And by the tail I yanked him out
And stamped him dead, for who would choose
To leave alive a sin?

The pale rose died of grief. My heel
Had killed its darling foe,
Worm that cuddles in the heart
To ravish it. If worm not tell
How should rose its fairness know?

KAY SMITH

1911–

'When a girl looks down'

When a girl looks down out of her cloud of hair
And gives her breast to the child she has borne,
All the suns and the stars that the heavens have worn
Since the first magical morning
Rain through her milk in each fibre and cell of her darling.

Hand baring the gift touches the hidden spring,
Source of all gifts, the womb of creation;
From the wide-open door streams the elation
Shaping all things, itself shapeless as air,

That models the nipple of girl, of bud, the angel
Forms unscrolling their voices over fields of winter,
That whittles the ray of a star to a heart's splinter
For one lost in his palace of breath on the frozen hill,
Flying the big-bellied moon for a sail,

And releases the flood of girl, of bud, of the horn
Whose music starts on a morning journey.
In mother, child and all, the One-in-the-many
Gathers me nearer to be born.

WILFRED WATSON

1911–

In the Cemetery of the Sun

For the first Monday of my week
Of darkness came May's last month. October
Wrath of Mayspring breathed on a smoulder
Of chrysanthemum, till it was dark
Shrivel, till it was the first sun
Of frost, till the cold of my fever
Breathed in the octave and after
Of the saintspring and feast of May,
Dry and dry its weather of leaves,
Dry and cold and dry its flower,
In the toward and paltry of death's unnecessary

There stood the skullbrow of my death's
Hill (and I saw seven partridge
In a brown apparition walk across
My grave of grass, my prairie of grave,
Birds of the earth made gross for winter,
Their fat breast bosomed in the sun's
Light, though the darkness of my hill was
Fat behind them, as they walked across
My morning and went) till my last day

Sang into my eyes. In the cemetery of the sun below
All the houses of the living were tombs;
And I saw Calgary a hill of tombstones
Rising under a coast of mountains
Washed in the cold of my sun of cloud.
When I walked to the wither of my day
In this city where every backyard had
Its cross and clothesline white and sere
With serecloths shining in the sun
Of my first despair of resurrection

Came my first Monday of darkness. It
Was the week's hanging and drying noon.
All the drought of my bones was for water.
And the ghosts of my people flapped about
Me in this washday blow and weather.
But though I bent in the drown of sun
To the mutter of sleeve and sheet
I could not find heart or answer
To answer that morning the winter
Upstart and May of this October
Wording me even to the spring of doom.

A Contempt for Dylan Thomas

sir Thomas, stark green until he crept acurl
into the bed of marriage, put ripeness on
in the soft white embraces of a girl,
misliked the very thought of such conjunction
and wished that we could love like plants and trees
joined by the trade of winds and hairs of bees.

poor Turleygod Thomas, his images askew
when men were making things of men, would hint
(being afraid no heaven can be true)
that thinghood is the heaven of the saint,
that man, poor gull, must wet his burning wings
and sink them in the sea of peaceful things.

o ragged Thomas, to stones, flowers, fire
believing, may not stones lie, fire fever in its flame,
and trees endure an agony of flower?
can we, to comprehend and feel its shame
creep into the full bosom of a stone
too dull to speak and make its hurt sense known?

IRVING LAYTON

1912–

The Swimmer

The afternoon foreclosing, see
The swimmer plunges from his raft,
Opening the spray corollas by his act of war –
The snake heads strike
Quickly and are silent.

Emerging see how for a moment
A brown weed with marvellous bulbs,
He lies imminent upon the water
While light and sound come with a sharp passion
From the gonad sea around the Poles
And break in bright cockle-shells about his ears.

He dives, floats, goes under like a thief
Where his blood sings to the tiger shadows
In the scentless greenery that leads him home,
A male salmon down fretted stairways
Through underwater slums. . . .

Stunned by the memory of lost gills
He frames gestures of self-absorption
Upon the skull-like beach;
Observes with instigated eyes
The sun that empties itself upon the water,
And the last wave romping in
To throw its boyhood on the marble sand.

Composition in Late Spring

When Love ensnares my mind unbidden
                    I am lost in the usual way

On a crowded street or avenue
Where I am lord of all the marquees,
And the traffic cop moving his lips
Like a poet composing
Whistles a discovery of sparrows
About my head.

My mind, full of goats and pirates
And simpler than a boy's,
I walk through a forest of white arms
That embrace me like window-shoppers;
Friends praise me like a Turkish delight
Or a new kind of suspender
And children love me
Like a story.

Conscience more flat than cardboard
Over the gap in a sole,
I avoid the fanatic whose subway
Collapsed in his brain;
There's a sinking, but the madonna
Who clings to my hairlock
Is saved: on shore the damned ones
Applaud with the vigour of bees.

The sparrows' golden plummeting
From fearful rooftop
Shows the flesh dying into sunshine.
Fled to the green suburbs, Death
Lies scared to death under a heap of bones.
Beauty buds from mire,
And I, a singer in season, observe
Death is a name for beauty not in use.

No one is more happy, none can do more tricks.
The sun melts like butter
Over my sweetcorn thoughts;
And, at last, both famous and good

I'm a Doge, a dog
At the end of a terrace
Where poems like angels like flakes of powder
Quaver above my prickling skin.

The Birth of Tragedy

And me happiest when I compose poems.
Love, power, the huzza of battle
are something, are much;
yet a poem includes them like a pool
water and reflection.
In me, nature's divided things –
tree, mould on tree –
have their fruition;
I am their core. Let them swap,
bandy, like a flame swerve
I am their mouth; as a mouth I serve.

And I observe how the sensual moths
big with odour and sunshine
dart into the perilous shrubbery;
or drop their visiting shadows
upon the garden I one year made
of flowering stone to be a footstool
for the perfect gods:
who, friends to the ascending orders,
will sustain this passionate meditation
and call down pardons
for the insurgent blood.

A quiet madman, never far from tears,
I lie like a slain thing
under the green air the trees
inhabit, or rest upon a chair
towards which the inflammable air
tumbles on many robins' wings;

noting how seasonably
leaf and blossom uncurl
and living things arrange their death,
while someone from afar off
blows birthday candles for the world.

The Fertile Muck

There are brightest apples on those trees
but until I, fabulist, have spoken
they do not know their significance
or what other legends are hung like garlands
on their black boughs twisting
like a rumour. The wind's noise is empty.

Nor are the winged insects better off
though they wear my crafty eyes
wherever they alight. Stay here, my love;
you will see how delicately they deposit
me on the leaves of elms
or fold me in the orient dust of summer.

And if in August joiners and bricklayers
are thick as flies around us
building expensive bungalows for those
who do not need them, unless they release
me roaring from their moth-proofed cupboards
their buyers will have no joy, no ease.

I could extend their rooms for them without cost
and give them crazy sundials
to tell the time with, but I have noticed
how my irregular footprint horrifies them
evenings and Sunday afternoons:
they spray for hours to erase its shadow.

How to dominate reality? Love is one way;
imagination another. Sit here

beside me, sweet; take my hard hand in yours.
We'll mark the butterflies disappearing over the hedge
 with tiny wristwatches on their wings:
our fingers touching the earth, like two Buddhas.

The Bull Calf

The thing could barely stand. Yet taken
from his mother and the barn smells
he still impressed with his pride,
with the promise of sovereignty in the way
his head moved to take us in.
The fierce sunlight tugging the maize from the ground
licked at his shapely flanks.
He was too young for all that pride.
I thought of the deposed Richard II.

'No money in bull calves,' Freeman had said.
The visiting clergyman rubbed the nostrils
now snuffing pathetically at the windless day.
'A pity,' he sighed.
My gaze slipped off his hat toward the empty sky
that circled over the black knot of men,
over us and the calf waiting for the first blow.

Struck,
the bull calf drew in his thin forelegs
as if gathering strength for a mad rush . . .
tottered . . . raised his darkening eyes to us,
and I saw we were at the far end
of his frightened look, growing smaller and smaller
till we were only the ponderous mallet
that flicked his bleeding ear
and pushed him over on his side, stiffly,
like a block of wood.

Below the hill's crest
the river snuffled on the improvised beach.

We dug a deep pit and threw the dead calf into it.
It made a wet sound, a sepulchral gurgle,
as the warm sides bulged and flattened.
Settled, the bull calf lay as if asleep,
one foreleg over the other,
bereft of pride and so beautiful now,
without movement, perfectly still in the cool pit,
I turned away and wept.

Cain

Taking the air rifle from my son's hand,
I measured back five paces, the Hebrew
In me, narcissist, father of children,
Laid to rest. From there I took aim and fired.
The silent ball hit the frog's back an inch
Below the head. He jumped at the surprise
Of it, suddenly tickled or startled
(He must have thought) and leaped from the wet sand
Into the surrounding brown water. But
The ball had done its mischief. His next spring
Was a miserable flop, the thrust all gone
Out of his legs. He tried – like Bruce – again,
Throwing out his sensitive pianist's
Hands as a dwarf might or a helpless child.
His splash disturbed the quiet pondwater
And one old frog behind his weedy moat
Blinking, looking self-complacently on.
The lin's surface at once became closing
Eyelids and bubbles like notes of music
Liquid, luminous, dropping from the page
White, white-bearded, a rapid crescendo
Of inaudible sounds and a crones' whispering
Backstage among the reeds and bulrushes
As for an expiring Lear or Oedipus.

But Death makes us all look ridiculous.

Consider this frog (dog, hog, what you will)
Sprawling, his absurd corpse rocked by the tides
That his last vain spring had set in movement.
Like a retired oldster, I couldn't help sneer,
Living off the last of his insurance:
Billows – now crumbling – the premiums paid.
Absurd, how absurd. I wanted to kill
At the mockery of it, kill and kill
Again – the self-infatuate frog, dog, hog,
Anything with the stir of life in it,
Seeing the dead leaper, Chaplin-footed,
Rocked and cradled in this afternoon
Of tranquil water, reeds, and blazing sun,
The hole in his back clearly visible
And the torn skin a blob of shadow
Moving when the quiet poolwater moved.
O Egypt, marbled Greece, resplendent Rome,
Did you also finally perish from a small bore
In your back you could not scratch? And would
Your mouths open ghostily, gasping out
Among the murky reeds, the hidden frogs,
We climb with crushed spines toward the heavens?

When the next morning I came the same way
The frog was on his back, one delicate
Hand on his belly, and his white shirt front
Spotless. He looked as if he might have been
A comic; tapdancer apologizing
For a fall, or an Emcee, his wide grin
Coaxing a laugh from us for an aside
Or perhaps a joke we didn't quite hear.

El Gusano

From the place where I was sitting
I watched the weary stone-splitters
Building a road to blot out the sun;

And seeing their sweating bodies
In the merciless, mid-day heat
I wished I could do it for them:
Turn it out like a light, I mean.
And I almost rose up to do so
When my eyes suddenly picked out
A strange, never-before-seen worm
Making its way on the dried leaves.
It had a rich, feudal colour,
Reddish-brown like the Spanish soil
And knew its way among the stones
So plentiful in Alicante.
I love lizards and toads; spiders, too
And all humped and skin-crinkled creatures
But most in love I am with worms.
These sages never ask to know
A man's revenue or profession;
And it's not at antecedents
Or at class that they draw their line
But will dine with impartial relish
On one who splits stones or sells fish
Or, if it comes to that, a prince
Or a generalissimo.
Bless the subversive, crawling dears
Who here are the sole underground
And keep alive in the country
The idea of democracy.
I gave it a mock-Falangist
Salute and it crawled away; or
Was it the stone-splitters frightened
The worm off and the brittle noise
Of almond-pickers? It vanished
Under a dusty dried-up leaf
For a restful snooze in the ground
But I imagine it now tunnelling
Its hard way to Andalusia
Faithful to the colourful soil
Under the villas and motels

Of those whose bankers let them stow
Ancient distinctions and treasure
In the rear of their foreign cars.
O plundered, sold-out, and lovely
Shore of the Mediterranean:
This worm shall knit the scattered plots
Of your traduced, dismembered land;
And co-worker of wave and wind,
Proud, untiring apostle to
The fragrant and enduring dust,
Carry its political news
To Castile and to Aragon.

GEORGE JOHNSTON

1913–

War on the Periphery

Around the battlements go by
Soldier men against the sky,
Violent lovers, husbands, sons,
Guarding my peaceful life with guns.

My pleasures, how discreet they are!
A little booze, a little car,
Two little children and a wife
Living a small suburban life.

My little children eat my heart;
At seven o'clock we kiss and part,
At seven o'clock we meet again;
They eat my heart and grow to men.

I watch their tenderness with fear
While on the battlements I hear
The violent, obedient ones
Guarding my family with guns.

Music in the Air

What noise up there?
What but a duck in the moon-bright
Neck-sustaining air
Giving a quack to the night?

He makes the sky his pond and drowns the street
And drowns me too, homing on fishy feet
To where my doorway sucks its scaly mouth:
Heaven is north, and my drowned home is south,
And there my caverned coal fire covets me
Of the duck's night. Quack! in the dark, says he.

DOUGLAS LE PAN

1914–

Canoe-trip

What of this fabulous country
Now that we have it reduced to a few hot hours
And sun-burn on our backs?
On this south side the countless archipelagoes,
The slipway where titans sent splashing the last great glaciers;
And then up to the foot of the blue pole star
A wilderness,
The pinelands whose limits seem distant as Thule,
The millions of lakes once cached and forgotten,
The clearings enamelled with blueberries, rank silence about
  them;
And skies that roll all day with cloud-chimeras
To baffle the eye with portents and unwritten myths,
The flames of sunset, the lions of gold and gules.
Into this reservoir we dipped and pulled out lakes and rivers,
We strung them together and made our circuit.
Now what shall be our word as we return,
What word of this curious country?

It is good,
It is a good stock to own though it seldom pays dividends.
There are holes here and there for a gold-mine or a hydro-plant.
But the tartan of river and rock spreads undisturbed,
The plaid of a land with little desire to buy or sell.
The dawning light skirls out its independence;
At noon the brazen trumpets slash the air;
Night falls, the gulls scream sharp defiance;
Let whoever comes to tame this land, beware!
Can you put a bit to the lunging wind?
Can you hold wild horses by the hair?
Then have no hope to harness the energy here,
It gallops along the wind away.

But here are crooked nerves made straight,
The fracture cured no doctor could correct.
The hand and mind, reknit, stand whole for work;
The fable proves no cul-de-sac.
Now from the maze we circle back;
The map suggested a wealth of cloudy escapes;
That was a dream, we have converted the dream to act.
And what we now expect is not simplicity,
No steady breeze, or any surprise,
Orchids along the portage, white water, crimson leaves.
Content, we face again the complex task.

And yet the marvels we have seen remain.
We think of the eagles, of the fawns at the river bend,
The storms, the sudden sun, the clouds sheered downwards.
O so to move! With such immaculate decision!
O proudly as waterfalls curling like cumulus!

An Incident

Arrange the scene with only a shade of difference
And he would be a boy in his own native
And fern-fronded providence,
With a map in his hand, searching for a portage overgrown
With brush. Slim he is as a moccasin-flower
With his throat open
To the winds, to the four winds, quivering,
Who alone by the worm-holed flower of the rose-pink house
Bears the weight of this many-ringed, foreign noon,
Shadowless, vast and pitiless.
Notched by the wedge of his frown, it takes no notice.
Light that, alive, would be pungent with resin,
Sapless, now weighs and ponders like limestone.

What is he waiting for
As he studies a map the colour of his youth?
Time stops and whirs in his ear like a humming-bird

As he gazes this way and that
For someone to relieve him
For someone to break through the thicket of his isolation.

In the silence
The grasshoppers crackle and crumble the summer
Between their thin wings
And their singing thighs.
And his head has begun to sing,
To sing with the heat.
Stampeding, his blood butts him like a bull-calf.
How should one so young have learned how to wait?

Ah! there is the relief.
A stray round has caught him at the nape of the neck
And splayed him flat on the earth,
His blood flung wide as a sunburst.

And the pink house, that eavesdropped
Through smoke-blackened holes to each palpitation,
Recovering its reserve,
Sucks in unblemished stillness;
While the wise light with petrified foliage
Having disposed of this awkward animal tremor
Again stands superb as a temple.

The Nimbus

To dive for the nimbus on the sea-floor
   Or seek it in the sun
Calls for a plucky steeplejack
   Scaling the sky's giddy ocean
Or dolphin-hearted journeyman
To swim from the foundered sunburst's roar
   With lost treasure on his back.

Ocean that slovens and sidles in vast
   Indifference, hides

In its sludge a wreath of drowning bells.
  Who in those tricky tides
Or up the slippery daybreak's sides
Can grapple the spices of morning fast
  That waste on the listless swells?

Smothered beneath a lowering ceiling
  All cock-crow crispness dies.
Bleary hordes are afraid to wake
  Into the mists that rise
From a palsied swamp where a marsh-bird cries.
Stranger, reconquer the source of feeling
  For an anxious people's sake.

Plunder the mind's aerial cages
  Or the heart's deep catacombs.
O daring's virtuoso, tossed
  Where the furious sunlight foams
Or through the instinct's twilit glooms,
Return with the sunburst's glistering pledges
  As a garland for the lost.

A bittern rusting in the reeds
  Is startled, and through the mist
Whirs screaming. Now, if now only, come
  With the nimbus in your fist.
Strike, strike the rust like a rhapsodist
And burnish gold each throat that pleads
  For dawn's encomium.

R. A. D. FORD

1915–

Roadside near Moscow

Bent and heavy with rain,
Staggering in silence, profoundly
Occupied with the secret reconstruction
Of their balance, pine and tamarack
Trees, gathered in profane

Assembly to watch over the slow
Passing of the almost human-like
Column of prisoners, waiting for the snow
To fill in their tracks – strange
Judges of evil done

In many ways. Because I am not
Walking in chains, and am afraid
To look, lest by implication
Glance should be said guilty,
Unhappily turn my head

To the stale spectacle of the sun
Setting among the conifers.
And when it is gone, look down
For the column of men in vain –
In the thick arch of night

That has come suddenly,
Hobble my eyes to perceive
Nothing but the rain, turning
To snow, – all that I wish to see.

The Thieves of Love

Uncautiously, unheeding, thinking
Themselves alone, the lovers

Walk, firm in belief, under
The pine tree fringes of the wood,

Oblivious to the change
Of seasons worn in the cones
And needles, or the end
Of summer hidden in the sap.

Unperceiving, sad, unhuman,
We, trained from the years
Not to see, now see
From the moment happening

The startled flash of time,
The bough breaking underfoot,
To the sameness of infinity,
The oblivion of love.

And hope they will not
In any case turn round to cast
One last and suddenly
Disillusioned glance

At the camp-followers
Of love, and the trackers
And thieves of happiness,
Sodden in the underbrush.

PATRICK ANDERSON

1915–

Cold Colloquy

From *Poem on Canada*

What are you . . .? they ask, in wonder.
And she replies in the worst silence of all her woods:
I am Candida with the cane wind.

What are you . . .? they ask again, their mouths full of gum,
their eyes full of the worst silence of the worst winter in a hundred
  years
and the frames of their faces chipped round the skaters' picture –

What are you . . .? they ask.
And she replies: I am the wind that wants a flag.
I am the mirror of your picture
until you make me the marvel of your life.
Yes, I am one and none, pin and pine, snow and slow,
America's attic, an empty room,
a something possible, a chance, a dance
that is not danced. A cold kingdom.

Are you a dominion of them? they ask, scurrying
home on streetcars, skiing the hill's shoulder
and hurrying where the snow is heaping colder and colder.
Are you a dominion of them? they ask.
Most loyal and empirical, she says in ice ironic,
and subject of the king's most gratuitous modesty, she says.
What do you do then?
Lumbering is what I do and whitening is what I wheat,
but I am full of hills and sadness;
snow is where I drift and wave my winds
and as silence my doom, distance is my dream.

Mine are the violet tones of the logs in rivers,
my tallness is the tallness of the pines and the grain elevators
tubular by the scarps of coal, at Quebec.
My caves are the caves of ice but also the holes of Cartier
where the poor squat, numb with winter,
and my poverty is their rags and the prairies' drought.

What is the matter then . . .? they ask, and some are indifferent,
What is the matter then . . .? they ask.

The matter is the sections and the railways, she replies,
and the shouting lost by the way and the train's whistle
like wild-life in the night.
The matter is the promise that was never taken, she replies,
above your heads the cool and giant air
and the future aching round you like an aura –
land of the last town and the distant point,
land of the lumber track losing itself
petering out in the birches, the half-wish
turning back in the wastes of winter or slums
and the skiers lovely and lonely upon the hills
rising in domes of silence. The matter is
the skiers, she replies, athletically lonely,
drowsed in their delight, who hunt and haunt
the centres of their silence and excitement:
finding the cirrus on the high sierras
sluice down the dangers of their dear content –
the matter is being lost in a dream of motion
as larks are in their lights, or bees and flies
glued on the humpbacked honey of summertime.

What should we do then, what should we do . . .? they ask,
out of the factories rattling a new war,
on all the Sundays time has rocked to motion.
What should we do then . . .? they ask, English and French,
Ukrainians, Poles, Finns, at drugstore corners
of streets extended to the ultimate seas
of their defended but ambiguous city.

– Suffer no more the vowels of Canada
to speak of miraculous things with a cleft palate –
let the Canadian,
with glaciers in his hair, straddle the continent,
in full possession of his earth and north
dip down his foot and touch the New York lights
or stir the vegetable matter of the Bahamas
within the Carib gutter. Let
the skiers go with slogans of their eyes
to crowd a country whose near neighbourhood's
the iron kindness of the Russian coasts –
through deserts of snow or dreary wastes of city,
the empty or the emptily crowded North.

And see, she says, the salmon pointing home
from the vast sea, the petalled plethora
and unplumbed darkness of the sea, she says:
gliding along their silvery intuitions
like current on its cables, volt upon volt,
to flash at last, sparking the mountain falls
of Restigouche – spawning a silver million.

My Bird-wrung Youth

My bird-wrung youth began with the quick naked
voice in the morning, the crooked calling,
and closed in the quiet wave of the falling
wing, dropping down like an eyelid –
                    O syringing liquid
song on the bough of flight and at night, light failing,
                    the nested
                    kiss of the breasted

ones floating out to sleep in a cup of colours;
wren's flit and dimple, the shadowy wing of the curlew
spent between stone and fern in the hollow,
the barn-raftered swallow and far at sea the rider
                    gull on the billow

all night, all night kept sleep till steeply
 the pillow
 threw morning cockcrow
up in a column of straw and blood. In childhood
days opened like that, whistled and winked away,
but now with a harsher cry birds bury
my stolen heart deep in the wild orchard,
 and whether they prettily
play with the plucked bud here or marry
 a cloud, I
 am lost, am emptied

between two sizes of success. For, flocking
past ceiling and dream sailing, they drop down
to pick apart in a nimble and needled rain
my limbs in love with longing, yet still I long
 for my twin in the sun
they rise to, they almost form, to be born
 with a song
 in a seventh heaven!

And I alone in the ambivalence
of April's green and evil see them still
colonizing the intricately small
or flashing off into a wishing distance –
 their nearer syllables
peck through the webs of every loosening sense
 and in their tall
 flight's my betrayal.

Drinker

Loping and sloped with heat, face thatched and red,
hating his engine boots spraying mechanical pebbles
he slowly comes through the white blocked light to the
 fountain:
his shirt clinging about him wet and rose
hangs heavily in front with his chest's sour bracket.

He crouches then: he turns with a serious hand
the little wheel: hangs, freckles over the jet
rising in a crush of water towards his burning mouth:
his eyes are wide and grave, his act seems private,
and as his hand spreads on the green stained stone
his massive working throat is a column of pure love.

He tastes with the iron pipe the very roots of water
spreading under the ground, which in multitudinous dirt
and infinite threaded dark are purified –
he draws the long stalk of water up between his lips
and in his sandy mouth there bursts its melting flower.

P. K. PAGE

1916–

The Bands and the Beautiful Children

Band makes a tunnel of the open street
at first, hearing it;
seeing it, band becomes
high; brasses ascending on the strings of sun
build their own auditorium of light,
windows from cornets
and a dome of drums.

And always attendant on bands, the beautiful children,
white with running and innocence;
and the arthritic old
who, patient behind their windows
are no longer split by the quick yellow of imagination
or carried beyond their angular limits of distance.

But the children move
in the trembling building of sound,
sure as a choir
until band breaks and scatters,
crumbles about them and is made of men
tired and grumbling
on the straggling grass.

And the children, lost, lost,
in an open space,
remember the certainty of the anchored home
and cry on the unknown edge of their own city
their lips stiff from an imaginary trumpet.

Element

Feeling my face has the terrible shine of fish
caught and swung on a line under the sun

I am frightened held in the light that people make
and sink in darkness freed and whole again
as fish returned by dream into the stream.

Oh, running water is not rough: ruffled to eye,
to flesh it's flat and smooth; to fish
silken as children's hands in milk.

I am not wishful in this dream of immersion.
Mouth becomes full with darkness
and the shine, mottled and pastel, sounds its own note, not
the fake high treble thrown on resounding faces.

There are flowers – and this is pretty for the summer –
light on the bed of darkness; there are stones
that glisten and grow slime;
winters that question nothing, are a new
night for the passing movement of fine fins;
and quietly, by the reeds or the water fronds
something can cry without discovery.

Ah, in daylight the shine is single
as dime flipped or gull on fire or fish
silently hurt – its mouth alive with metal.

Summer

I grazed the green as I fell
and in my blood
the pigments flowed like sap.
All through my veins the green
made a lacey tree.
Green in my eye grew big as a bell
that gonged and struck
and in a whorl of green in my ear
it spun like a ball.

Orphaned at once that summer
having sprung
full grown and firm with green,
chorussed with fern.
Oh, how the lazy moths were soft upon
my feminine fingers,
how flowers foamed at my knees
all those green months.

Near reeds and rushes where the water lay
fat and lustred by the sun
I sang the green that was in my groin,
the green
of lily and maidenhair and fritillary
from the damp wood
of cedar and cypress from the slow hill,
and the song, stained with the stain of chlorophyll
was sharp as a whistle of grass
in my green blood.

The Stenographers

After the brief bivouac of Sunday,
their eyes, in the forced march of Monday to Saturday,
hoist the white flag, flutter in the snow storm of paper,
haul it down and crack in the midsun of temper.

In the pause between the first draft and the carbon
they glimpse the smooth hours when they were children –
the ride in the ice-cart, the ice-man's name,
the end of the route and the long walk home;

remember the sea where floats at high tide
were sea marrows growing on the scatter-green vine
or spools of grey toffee, or wasps' nests on water;
remember the sand and the leaves of the country.

Bell rings and they go and the voice draws their pencil
like a sled across snow; when its runners are frozen
rope snaps and the voice then is pulling no burden
but runs like a dog on the winter of paper.

Their climates are winter and summer – no wind
for the kites of their hearts – no wind for a flight;
a breeze at the most, to tumble them over
and leave them like rubbish – the boy-friends of blood.

In the inch of the noon as they move they are stagnant.
The terrible calm of the noon is their anguish;
the lip of the counter, the shapes of the straws
like icicles breaking their tongues are invaders.

Their beds are their oceans – salt water of weeping
the waves that they know – the tide before sleep;
and fighting to drown they assemble their sheep
in columns and watch them leap desks for their fences
and stare at them with their own mirror-worn faces.

In the felt of the morning the calico minded,
sufficiently starched, insert papers, hit keys,
efficient and sure as their adding machines;
yet they weep in the vault, they are taut as net curtains
stretched upon frames. In their eyes I have seen
the pin men of madness in marathon trim
race round the track of the stadium pupil.

BERTRAM WARR

1917–43

The Heart to Carry On

Every morning from this home
I go to the aerodrome.
And at evening I return
Save when work is to be done.
Then we share the separate night
Half a continent apart.

Many endure worse than we:
Division means by years and seas.
Home and lover are contained,
Even cursed within their breast.

Leaving you now, with this kiss
May your sleep tonight be blest,
Shielded from the heart's alarms
Until morning I return.
Pray tomorrow I may be
Close, my love, within these arms,
And not lie dead in Germany.

There are Children in the Dusk

Forget the dead, this time
Who are not glorious.
Their sacrifice builds to our crisis,
And the last war left us no sites
To raise our monuments.
We will not weep at unveilings;
Tenderness only confuses
The children who wait in the dusk.

ELDON GRIER

1917–

On the Subject of Waves . . .

Mountain teeth, tips of anemious rippled stone,
a glacier of white cloud settled into the tilting passages:

Are you there, Li?

Are you there in the mists, Li Po?

If I ring your two-change name against the massive greys
will you answer?
On this day and in this location can you see how it is
with us humans?

There are greens about me here, and the pressure of the
soft gloom,
animals in the rising fields.
Men I shall never see
stand in the doorways of their huts like true sentinels
of life.
There are chimneys behind me rolling up the first balls
of pale smoke.
A high plateau above, ceaselessly swept with tears of anemia,
before me, and always in my mind is the shape of peninsulas
as insistent as a black mirror.

The empty truck, traumatically still;
A score of men loosely grouped beneath a tree.
The stillness is the echo of an explosion!

I find the burlap square in the centre of the road
and I know that beneath it there is a dead child.

Is this what you meant by 'waves', Li Po?

View from a Window

The tenderness so hard to swallow
is partly the two flies settled in her hair.

Her mouth opens to the soothing air,
drools scabs curving down from its edges.

And her brother whom she holds shyly for me to admire . . .
the mess of mucus and the clinging feeding flies . . .
awake, a toxic film covers his eyes
shifting mechanically in patterns of escape.

Across the steeply climbing flat-faced street
at the six vertical ochre strips,
her older sisters, short skirts flaring from the hips,
emerge and blow away buoyant as wasps.

Beauty complicates the average squalor,
carries the unpredictable like fallout
into the brutal levels, burns about
the ruin and the green vine with its yearning.

She hangs around; she says she's eight.
Her name is tuned for ceremonial complaint;
mine is, that dozy flies can travel here without restraint
in the gentlest of hatchures.

In Memory of Garcia Lorca

Garcia Lorca,
Did you think
They'd let it go,
A flower in the lapel
Of perpetual mourning?
Did you guess
The brilliant words
Had made you alien
And (strangely)
Evil?

Granada let you die
Like any freak;

Forgot the day,
Forgot which pit it was.

Gypsies, farmers, generals,
Priests, tourists,
And the quiet rich,
Now pass blandly
Overhead.

Oiga hombre!
Ask around.
Somewhere,
Buried,
Is a silver skull.

Quebec

At steeplecock height
In a tousling wind,
Bands of tourists,
Ants in the spiral
Dimension of birds,
Stalk the pale
Ghosts of history.
Bet on each parroting guide
For signs of the dead.
But brother, nobody's home
Except the river
With its carnival of ships
And the dizzying miles.
Forget your books and cameras.
Dream you flew here
And that lunchtime never comes.
History is in the hotel lounges;
The delicate Wolfe,
Dying in a bed of flags,
Or Montcalm, propped in the backstage
Ruin of battle.

MIRIAM WADDINGTON

1917–

The Season's Lovers

In the daisied lap of summer
The lovers lay, they dozed
And lay in sun unending,
They lay in light, they slept
And only stirred
Each one to find the other's lips.
At times they sighed
Or spoke a word
That wavered on uneven breath,
He had no name and she forgot
The ransomed kingdom of her death.

When at last the sun went down
And chilly evening stained the fields,
The lovers rose and rubbed their eyes:
They saw the pale wash of grass
Heighten to metallic green
And spindly tongues of granite mauve
Lick up the milk of afternoon,
They gathered all the scattered light
Of daisies to one place of white,
And ghostly poets lent their speech
To the stillness of the air,
The lovers listened, each to each.

Into the solid wall of night,
The lovers looked, their clearer sight
Went through that dark intensity
To the other side of light.
The lovers stood, it seemed to them
They hung upon the world's rim –
He clung to self, and she to him;
He rocked her with his body's hymn

And murmured to her shuddering cry,
You are all states, all princes I,
And sang against her trembling limbs,
Nothing else is, he sang, *but I.*

They lifted the transparent lid
From world false and world true
And in the space of both they flew.
He found a name, she lost her death,
And summer lulled them in its lap
With leafy lullaby.
There they sleep unending sleep,
The lovers lie
He with a name, she free of death,
In a country hard to find
Unless you read love's double mind
Or invent its polar map.

Thou Didst Say Me

Late as last summer
thou didst say me, love
I choose you, you, only you.
oh the delicate del-
icate serpent of your lips
the golden lie bedazzled
me with wish and flash
of joy and I was fool.

I was fool, bemused
bedazed by summer, still
bewitched and wandering
in murmur hush in green-
ly sketched-in fields
I was, I was, so sweet
I was, so honied with
your gold of love and love
and still again more love.

late as last autumn
thou didst say me, dear
my doxy, I choose you and
always you, thou didst pledge
me love and through the red-
plumed weeks and soberly
I danced upon your words
and garlanded these
tender dangers.

year curves to ending now
and thou dost say me, wife
I choose another love, and oh
the delicate del-
icate serpent of your mouth
stings deep, and bitter
iron cuts and shapes
my death, I was so fool.

Green World Two

Locked in a glassy iceland lake
I was a child chinning myself
on reflected treetops.
Into my green world
winter shone and splashed
me real with light.

My summer gone,
the knob of light still turns
in that locked lake;
under the seal of ice
the cabined light still burns,
and the yellow haystacks flare
on underwater beaches.
Far above the snow
fills the falling world
to its topmost branches.

MARGARET AVISON

1918–

Perspective

A sport, an adventitious sprout
These eyeballs, that have somehow slipped
The mesh of generations since Mantegna?

Yet I declare, your seeing is diseased
That cripples space. The fear has eaten back
Through sockets to the caverns of the brain
    And made of it a sifty habitation.

We stand beholding the one plain
And in your face I see the chastening
Of its small tapering design
That brings up *punkt.*
    (The infinite, you say,
    Is an unthinkable – and pointless too –
    Extension of that *punkt.*)

But ho you miss the impact of that fierce
Raw boulder five miles off? You are not pierced
By that great spear of grass on the horizon?
    You are not smitten with the shock
        Of that great thundering sky?

Your law of optics is a quarrel
Of chickenfeet on paper. Does a train
Run pigeon-toed?

I took a train from here to Ottawa
On tracks that did not meet. We swelled and roared
Mile upon mightier mile, and when we clanged
Into the vasty station we were indeed
Brave company for giants.

Keep your eyes though,
You, and not I, will travel safer back
To Union station.
Your fear has me infected, and my eyes
That were my sport so long, will soon be apt
Like yours to press out dwindling vistas from
The massive flux massive Mantegna knew
And all its sturdy everlasting foregrounds.

Knowledge of Age

Knowledge of age
Begins in winter, a thin-railed whistling gate
Under sonorous pines,
A few shivering paces, and so far,
From the stone house and all its hearths.

A slow slow seethe
Of snow across banana branches
Illumined on a silk of sky
Distinctly green, although no arch is there
Or any stone or structure,
Is sino-savagery, gentler than any Italy's
(On endless terraces of wine-stained space
Only plump cherubs play).

So when, an afternoon bruised as November,
All in a park, nine small suede reindeer
Feed on green moss
And city's heaven sunders to a
Swift appropriate blue,
Memory of last year's summer shrivels
Without nostalgia or any
Salve or sanction.

Anatomist, make distinct this bone from the
Bone of the uncorrupted dead.

Tennis

Service is joy, to see or swing. Allow
All tumult to subside. Then tensest winds
Buffet, brace, viol and sweeping bow.

Courts are for love and volley. No one minds
The cruel elipse of service and return,
Dancing white galliardes at tape or net
Till point, on the wire's tip, or the long burn-
ing arc to nethercourt marks game and set.
Purpose apart, perched like an umpire, dozes,
Dreams golden balls whirring through indigo.
Clay blurs the whitewash but day still encloses
The albinos, bonded in their flick and flow.
Playing in musicked gravity, the pair
Score liquid Euclids in foolscaps of air.

Janitor Working on Threshold

Boot-soles and overalled haunches to the street,
kneeling –
bowed from the ivy-falling, darkly-bright
day-ceiling,
and from cool stone, green court inside –
prising some broken stripping loose, and all in
slow skill, plain sight,
working, till no one need be afraid of falling –

this street
and door in the final stilling
of all (of the one at the threshold with the rest)
recall the less than the least,
John, and the wings, and healing.

MARGARET AVISON

For Dr and Mrs Dresser

Your doctor, Lord,
from West Irian,
brought pictures of a leaf that served as plate,
and grubs, fat, silkily hirsute, that men
need there for nourishment.
Whoever speak your word
along that coast must share
that feast of fatness first
for love of you and them
who offer from your provenance their best.
The gorge that finds your natural good
in food that squirms is
given aptitude, surely, by grace. . . .

As that doctor, Lord,
learned to subsist, in order
to love first-hand, for you, and tell
how God, to His plain table
invites them too, and will
dwell among them who offer Him their all,
You, once for all,
offered and dwelt – you, fairest beyond call
of mortal imagining:
here, taking on yourself not only
our spoiled flesh, but the lonely
rot of the rebel, of the solitary,
of all not-God on earth, for all
who claim, in all your range of time. And still
without one queasy tremor, you could wholly
swallow our death, take on our
lumpish wingless being, darkened out
to cold and night – except for
the timeless love
even for us, my Lord.

And having suffered us to glut
the pure well-spring, and having
plumbed even hell, for us, you could
come back, in flesh, living, and
open out the shaft and sweep
of clarity and scope,
flooding us with your risen radiance,
can bid us, in turn, o gentle Saviour:
'take, eat –
live'.

. . . Person, or A Hymn on and to the Holy Ghost

How should I find speech
to you, the self-effacing
whose other self was seen
alone by the only one,

to you whose self-knowing
is perfect, known to him,
seeing him only, loving
with him, yourself unseen?

Let the one you show me
ask you, for me,
you, all but lost in
the one in three,

to lead *my* self, effaced
in the known Light,
to be in him released
from facelessness,

so that where you
(unseen, unguessed, liable
to grievous hurt) would go
I may show him visible.

LOUIS DUDEK

1918–

The Jungle

Time has its ends and its beginnings –
  leaf-end and stems, skin and liver –
through which the rhythm passes,
  a drum-beat in a jungle silence,
somewhere in the trees the shriek
  of a wild bird shattered by claws,
somewhere the big cats mating, crying
  in pain, possibly in delight,
and the silence is endless, listening to the drums
  day after day with a new beginning,
day after day anguish, possibly pleasure,
  but beyond that the perfect white of the sky
waiting above the world for the movement to cease,
  to be absorbed in the folds of its sea,
to be drowned in space where all that was
  is sound in a deaf ear, fear in a forgotten dream.

The Pomegranate

The jewelled mine of the pomegranate, whose hexagons of honey
The mouth would soon devour but the eyes eat like a poem,
Lay hidden long in its hide, a diamond of dark cells
Nourished by tiny streams which crystallized into gems.

The seeds, nescient of the world outside, or of passionate teeth,
Prepared their passage into light and air, while tender roots
And branches dreaming in the cell-walled hearts of plants
Made silent motions such as recreate both men and fruits.

There, in a place of no light, shone that reddest blood,
And without a word of order, marshalled those grenadiers:

Gleaming without a sun – what art where no eyes were! –
Till broken by my hand, this palace of unbroken tears.

To wedding bells and horns howling down an alley,
Muffled, the married pair in closed caravan ride;
And then, the woman grown in secret, shining white,
Unclothed, mouth to mouth he holds his naked bride.

And there are days, golden days, when the world starts to life,
When streets in the sun, boys, and battlefields of cars,
The colours on a banister, the vendors' slanting stands
Send the pulse pounding on like the bursting of meteors –

As now, the fruit glistens with a mighty grin,
Conquers the room; and, though in ruin, to its death
Laughs at the light that wounds it, wonderfully red,
So that its awful beauty stops the greedy breath.

And can this fact be made, so big, of the body, then?
And is beauty bounded all in its impatient mesh?
The movement of the stars is that, and all their light
Secretly bathed the world, that now flows out of flesh.

From *Europe*

31

The ignorant present has scribbled over the past
at Winchester;
an American goon
painted on the door
saying 'yak yak' to all this
rectangular, proud English Gothic.

At first there was nothing, the beginning
was hardest, then what they made
was made out of what they had begun.

No matter. The present is shaped out of the first
shaped stones,
from Stonehenge to this.

They have written their initials
beside the dead. New Englishmen
and Americans, make goons
on golden doors.

It is all flowers within
and fluted stems,
'Music,' you said, and 'One cannot believe,'
I said,
'That it is of stone,' such intricate
articulations
of white bone, and terrible black
medieval magic.

But there is nothing,
nothing in the 19th century additions.
The recent
cemetery sculpture looks silly
beside the older, somber, Norman Gothic
that did not even try to be beautiful.
Only true.
To what? Consider for instance
the harrowing tomb of Richard Fox
showing his body
lacerated by suffering and death,
there to tell you
– do not be too gay, even if God
doesn't particularly matter,
the bones remain, they are the cathedral.

But several tourists
have scrawled their names
on the breast of Richard Fox
just where the skeleton comes through the skin.

Let these additions remain
in Winchester
Perhaps time will prove
such fools, like sculptured animals
belong here after all.
They would have had no stone
to write so plainly on, if death had not offered them
its bony breast.

95

The sea retains such images
in her ever-unchanging waves;
for all her infinite variety, and the forms,
inexhaustible, of her loves,
she is constant always in beauty,
which to us need be nothing more
than a harmony with the wave on which we move.
All ugliness is a distortion
of the lovely lines and curves
which sincerity makes out of hands
and bodies moving in air.
Beauty is ordered in nature
as the wind and sea
shape each other for pleasure; as the just
know, who learn of happiness
from the report of their own actions.

Dawn

I woke up with morning yawning in my mouth
with laughter overflowing a tea-kettle spout;
I woke up with apples rolling in my belly
in a barn, and six thousand fireflies going south.

I had just left a sun from whose milk-white aura
shining in speckled sacraments on teacup and floor

the black wings of the dawn-fly roared like dreams
and fought with two suns on a pin, changing colour:

giving its light to Day, today and many days!
The timeless bug out of a light that never fades
flew out and fluttered like a monkey clapping hands,
and it stood still, so beautiful it left me crazed.

Mouths

Pendulous mouth, you flap in a wind
            on a space-washed skull,
make a wilderness of sound
        brlaa
            brlaa frloo

flapping mouths
        on wind-swept heads –
until two cross to close the gap
between all art and artery, heart and the empty world

        lubb lubbu luvbl
            aluvu

close each other with a skill or will
under that spell
to loose themselves into each other,
            then turn to lose themselves
in that greater mouth
        nothing can still or fill.

ALFRED PURDY

1918–

At Roblin Lake

Did any one plan this?
Set up the co-ordinates
Of experiment to bring about
An ecology of near and distant
Batrachian nightingales?
Each with a frog in his throat,
Rehearsing the old springtime pap
About the glories of copulation.
If not I'd be obliged if
The accident would unhappen.

The pike and bass are admirably silent
About such things, and keep their
Erotic moments *a mensa et thoro*
In cold water. After which, I suppose,
Comes the non-judicial separation.
Which makes them somewhat misogynists –
Frogs are ignorant about the delusion and snare
Women represent – they brag and boast
Epicene, while piscene culture doesn't.

This tangential backyard universe
I inhabit with sidereal aplomb,
Though troubled with midnight debate
By frog theologians, bogged
Down in dialectics and original
Sin of discursiveness
(The god of boredom at one remove,
Discreetly subsidized on wooden plates).
This walking-morning I make a shore-capture,
With hands – having no air rifle.

Hold the chill, musical antibody
A moment with breath held,
Thinking of spores, spermatozoa, seed,
Housed in this cold progenitor,
Transmitting to some future species
What the wall said to Belshazzar.
And, wondering at myself, experiencing
For this bit of green costume jewellery
A nescient, obscure love.

Wilderness Gothic

Across Roblin Lake, two shores away,
they are sheathing the church spire
with new metal. Someone hangs in the sky
over there from a piece of rope,
hammering and fitting God's belly-scratcher,
working his way up along the spire
until there's nothing left to nail on –
Perhaps the workman's faith reaches beyond:
touches intangibles, wrestles with Jacob,
replacing rotten timber with pine thews,
pounds hard in the great cave of the sky,
contends heroically with difficult problems
of gravity, sky navigation and mythopoeia,
his volunteer time and labour donated to God,
minus sick benefits of course on a non-union job –

Fields around are yellowing into harvest,
nestling and fingerling are sky and water borne,
death is yodeling quiet in green woodlots,
and bodies of three young birds have disappeared
in the sub-surface of the new country highway –

That picture is incomplete, part left out
that might alter the whole Dürer landscape:
gothic ancestors peer from medieval sky,

dour faces trapped in photograph albums escaping
to clop down iron roads with matched greys:
work-sodden wives groping inside their flesh
for what keeps moving and changing and flashing
beyond and past the long frozen Victorian day.
A sign of fire and brimstone? A two-headed calf
born in the barn last night? A sharp female agony?
An age and a faith moving into transition,
the dinner cold and new-baked bread a failure,
deep woods shiver and water drops hang pendant,
double yolked eggs and the house creaks a little –
Something is about to happen. Leaves are still.
Two shores away, a man hammering in the sky.
Perhaps he will fall.

The Sculptors

Going thru cases and cases
of Eskimo sculpture
returned from Frobisher
because they said it wasn't
good enough for sale
to T. Eaton Co. Ltd.
Getting itchy excelsior packing
inside my shirt and searching
for one good carving
one piece that says 'I AM'
to keep a southern promise
One 6-inch walrus (tusk broken)
cribbage board (ivory inlay gone)
dog that has to be labeled dog
polar bear (only three bear paws)
what might be a seal (minus flipper)
and I'm getting tired of this
looking for something
not knowing what it is
But I guess they got tired too

looking for rabbit or bear
with blisters from carving tools
dime-sized and inflating
into quarters on their fingers
waiting
for walrus or white whale
under the ice floes to
flop alive on their lap
with twitching faces unready
to taste the shoe blacking
carvers use
for stone polish
I'm a little ashamed of myself
for being impatient with them
but there must be something
there must be something
one piece that glows
one slap-happy idiot seal
alien to the whole seal nation
one anthropomorphic walrus
singing Hallelujah I'm a bum
in a whiskey baritone
but they're all flawed
broken
          bent
                    misshapen
failed animals
with vital parts missing
And I have a sudden vision
of the carvers themselves
in this broken sculpture
as if the time & the place & me
had clicked into brief alignment
and a switch pulled
so that I can see and feel
what it was like to be them
the tb out-patients
failed hunters

who make a noise at the wrong time
or think of something else
at the trigger moment
and shine their eyes
into a continual tomorrow
the losers and failures
who never do anything right
and never will
the unlucky ones
always on the verge
of a tremendous discovery
who finally fail to deceive
even themselves as time begins
to hover around them
the old the old the old
who carve in their own image
of maimed animals
and I'd like to buy every damn case

– *at Pangnirtung.*

RAYMOND SOUSTER

1921–

The Day before Christmas

My best Christmases
are all behind me. Grandmother
lifting the done-to-perfection bird
grease-dripping from the pan. My brother

and I Xmas morning
out of bed at six-thirty. I suppose
the house shivered to the sudden sharp
tearing of gift-wrap by excited fingers.

This Christmas Eve mid-afternoon
too many years later, I wander downtown,
feeling worse than most drunks
set adrift from their office parties.

Birks' windows bulge and glow
with the totally conspicuous. There's something
fairy-queer about coloured lights
hung above the stink of bus exhausts.

Every store hums, an angry honey-hive,
as if wartime and rationing were back.
I picture patient clerks behind counters
walking on what they can't believe are feet.

Skaters on the fancy rink at City Hall
seem impatient of old waltzes. They dart,
sudden bright goldfish below Revell's
scooped clam-shells blinking underwater light.

My heart's with the skaters, though my mood
is more with Adam Beck, bronzed sober head

splitting the traffic of the Avenue,
where on that Republic's black Consul door I see

or seem to see a holly wreath hung, through which
napalm-skinned face and dying eyes stare out
at me, this city, and core-rotted world,
to riddle us with bleeding, gaping questions.

The Six-Quart Basket

The six-quart basket
one side gone
half the handle torn off

sits in the centre of the lawn
and slowly fills up
with the white fruits of the snow.

Where the Blue Horses

The street is quiet,
the noise through the wall is stilled,
the little cat curled up on the chair,
radio turned off, milk bottles outside the door.

And for now
nothing but sleep and dreams and thoughts of sleep,
not even love keep us awake tonight

as we sink into that strange land
where the blue horses toss
riderless and proud.

RAYMOND SOUSTER

Flight of the Roller Coaster

Once more around should do it, the man confided . . .

and sure enough, when the roller-coaster reached the peak
of the giant curve above me, screech of its wheels
almost drowned out by the shriller cries of the riders,

instead of the dip and plunge with its landslide of screams,
it rose in the air like a movieland magic carpet,
        some wonderful bird,

and without fuss or fanfare swooped slowly across
        the amusement park,
over Spook's Castle, ice-cream booths, shooting-gallery.
        And losing no height

made the last yards above the beach, where the cucumber-cool
brakeman in the last seat saluted
a lady about to change from her bathing-suit.

Then, as many witnesses reported, headed leisurely
        out over the water,
disappearing all too soon behind a low-flying flight of clouds.

ELI MANDEL

1922–

Job

Combination of Wagner and burlesque,
Denuded and bemused, like that fat beast
Leviathan, rolled on a beach of time he wears
Time like the ribboned colour of his wars,
Musing on wrecks and harbours.
A waste of middle ages rolls around
His corseted fat mind.
                    This structure stays
A raving skeleton
Constructing puzzled strictures for his God.

David

all day the gopher-killing boys
    their sling-shot arms
        their gopher-cries

the king insisting
    my poetry must stop

I have written nothing since May

instead
    walk among the boys
gopher-blood on their stretched
hands
    murder will end murder
the saying goes, someone must
do something about the rodents
and poems do not:
                    even the doctors

admit that it's plague
ask me about my arms
look
at my shadow hanging
like a slingshot

the world turns like a murderous stone
my forehead aching with stars

Phaeton

The giant wink in a clown's cheek
Shrinks the flared noon of his eye
And then it opens, moony and alarmed,
And spins concentric circles
Like a cartoon of stunned cat
Eye-struck by perpetual brickbats.

The snuff and puff of lung stuff
Wreathes the bright neck, the flashing mane,
The wide nostrils of a painted horse.

I saw this on a parchment once,
Eye, horse, and windy cheek,
Or sat that horse as frightened boy
And felt the sun go round and round
And take me with him by the ten taut reins
Of my skinned and burning hands.

Merits of Laughter and Lust

In this green world budged by the round shoulder
Of the infamous sky, sometimes even badgers
Are jovial; not everything is either digging
Or superior as the lifting cloud, the smile

Of the efficient harlot after the loveless act.
Madman Smart believed there are angels in flowers
And gems shining lightly in the depths of mines,
And wiser Ovid knew that lust is tough,
Survives scorn. So after Phaeton wrecked it,
Jove built Arcady again, and so today I love
The white round shoulder of the distant sky.

JAMES REANEY

1926–

The Katzenjammer Kids

With porcupine locks
And faces which, when
More closely examined,
Are composed of measle-pink specks,
These two dwarf imps,
The Katzenjammer Kids,
Flitter through their Desert Island world.
Sometimes they get so out of hand
That a blue Captain
With stiff whiskers of black wicker
And an orange Inspector
With a black telescope
Pursue them to spank them
All through that land
Where cannibals cut out of brown paper
In cardboard jungles feast and caper,
Where the sea's sharp waves continually
Waver against the shore faithfully
And the yellow sun above is thin and flat
With a collar of black spikes and spines
To tell the innocent childish heart that
It shines
And warms (see where she stands and stammers)
The dear fat mother of the Katzenjammers.
Oh, for years and years she has stood
At the window and kept fairly good
Guard over the fat pies that she bakes
For her two children, those dancing heartaches.
Oh, the blue skies of that funny paper weather!
The distant birds like two eyebrows close together!
And the rustling paper roar
Of the waves
Against the paper sands of the paper shore!

JAMES REANEY

The Horn

What is the horn that the dawn holds,
A soft shrill horn of feathers,
Cold as the dew on the grass by the paths,
Warm as the fire in the match in the box.
When this horn blows, in a sky of the sun
There rises our green star of earth
And the four evangelists who've borne
Thy bed down through the night
Now leave thee still thine eyes to see
The sun's separation of shadows.

Neither capons nor pullets nor hens
Can wake the sun and the world;
Only the prophets of the Old Testament
Huge old cocks, all speckled and barred,
Their wings like ragged pages of sermons,
Only they from their roosts in the henhouse
Can rouse the bread from its oven-sleep,
Raise the smoke from the haunted chimney.

Fierce old cock whose eyes look blind
So glaring and inspired are they,
Who live in this dungeon of cramp and dirt;
Fierce old fowl with shaking red wattles
Surrounding a beak like a kernel of wheat,
A yellow beak, plump, twisted and sharp
Which opens, hinged and prizing cry,
To show the sun's fistful of golden darts.

The Chough

The chough, said a dictionary,
Is a relation of the raven
And a relative of the crow.
It's nearly extinct,

But lingers yet
In the forests about Oporto.
So read I as a little child
And saw a young Chough in its nest,
Its very yellow beak already tasting
The delicious eyes
Of missionaries and dead soldiers;
Its wicked mind already thinking
Of how it would line its frowsy nest
With the gold fillings of dead men's teeth.
When I grew older I learned
That the chough, the raven and the crow
That rise like a key signature of black sharps
In the staves and music of a scarlet sunset
Are not to be feared so much
As that carrion bird, within the brain,
Whose name is Devouring Years,
Who gobbles up and rends
All odds and ends
Of memory, good thoughts and recollections
That one has stored up between one's ears
And whose feet come out round either eye.

The Oracular Portcullis

Illyria's hair fell down
Like a long golden answer
To a question in long division.
Gradually she let her saucer down
Crushing the invisible column
Of time and space beneath
Into a gently wounded saucer
And slowly the white portcullis rose,
The cruel ivory portcullis of her mouth
That had closed on both victims and visitors:
Many poached eggs and pieces of toast,
Duchess of Oldenburg apples,

And oceans of broth and soup.
Slowly Illyria made
Her delirious epigram:
'It is surely a well-known fact,
My dear,
That women are concave,
And men are convex?'
Thus spake Illyria; this question she posed,
Then quite quickly her portcullis closed.

From *A Suit of Nettles*
(September Eclogue)

The Drunken Preacher's Sermon

Lo, it was the last supper, I leader from gutter
Tell you tall and short tinkery folks gathered.
What did those white souls eat while their Lord talked:
I don't know indeed I don't, maybe sandwiches.
And He said haughtily head up to the twelve,
'I'll ask you assafoetidae again I will,
Isn't there one, one disciple with the spunk to betray me?'
They all fumbled their food, fed themselves slowly.
'Otherwise you see all my work ought in value is.'
'I will,' quavered weakly woefully poor Judas,
Runty little redhaired man runaway parents from him.
'I'll go through with ghoulish Holy Ghost necessary job.'
Even then at the end of it elder tree saw he.
His death, his Lord's death held at Lord's supper.
So you've all certainly betrayed him so you've done
Something for him by my bottle faith fiddle de dee you have.

PHYLLIS WEBB

1927–

Rilke

Rilke, I speak your name I throw it away
with your angels, your angels, your statues
and virgins, and a horse in a field held
at the hoof by wood. I cannot take so much
tenderness, tenderness, snow falling like lace
over your eyes year after year as the poems
receded, roses, the roses, sinking in snow
in the distant mountains.

Go away with your women to Russia or take them
to France, and take them or don't the poet is
in you, the spirit, they love that
(I met one in Paris, her death leaning outward,
death in all forms. The letters you'd sent her,
she said, stolen from a taxi.)

Rilke.
Clowns and angels held your compassion.
You could sit in a room saying nothing,
nothing. Your admirers thought you were there,
a presence, a wisdom. But you had to leave
everyone once, once at least. That was your
hardness.

This page is a shadowed hall in Duino Castle.
Echoes. The echoes.
I don't know why I'm here.

D. G. JONES

1929–

Northern Water Thrush

The bird walks by the shore
untouched by the falling sun
which crashes in the alders.

Lilting on delicate feet
among the dry reeds, the washed
and broken skeletons of trees,

he moves through his broken world
as one, alone surviving, moves
through the rubble of a recent war:

a world of silence but for the sound
of water tapping on the stones,
a drag of wind in the pine.

Grey with his yellow, fluted breast
he dips and halts, a string of notes
limned on the stillness of a void:

the stillness of the early spring
when new suns prepare
like new buds in the leafless air

a pristine world, the old
calligraphy of living things
having been destroyed.

But though he walks magnificent
upon the littered shore, holding
the moment with his poise,

he too will whiten with the days,
and the flawed human world
return with his delicate bone.

Poem for Good Friday

The green of the cedars is unlike
Any other green – they have been washed
By the wind, which now moves the clouds,
Piled like craggy props for Easter,
Into another part of the sky.
There will be no more snow.

The yellow of the starling's beak
Is like no other yellow – it neither
Gleams nor is dull; it proclaims
The late sunlight against the certain black.
There will be no suffering and no joy,
Only these two colours on a bruised sky.

The leafless branches of the trees
So proliferate against the broken clouds
That every twisted crucifix becomes
Only a limb. This is the earth where once
Men hung a man called Christ
On two planks. The starling drops in the wind.

The bottom of a pail is broken through.
An ancient house has gone to ruin.
There are no more metaphors, only
The green of the cedars, the yellow
Horn of the starling's beak, each
In the wind a part of April, now.

D. G. JONES

Boy in the Lamont Poetry Room, Harvard

His mouth babbling under the earphones,
Rocked by a rhetoric I cannot hear –

Who should be surprised if, suddenly,
He flew into the air, disappeared

In one feathered burst, Thoth,
Wild with declamation – if he left

Us standing, dumb, more or less stable,
Like so many cows, Chagall's, in a shaken world?

Annunciation

Snow has come back to make of weeds
A window-shopper's garden, frail
Easter Flowers for unbelievers.

But the sun is not the same, nor the hills.
And the silence when I stop the car
Is not the same, is a silence made

For a few birds, their thin
Aerial music. This is the coin
Flung against the brazen tower.

It is the confidence within (not
Of what endures) of what will be.
Distant. It transforms

This window to a world. Again.
The air is not just air, it is an arctic
Confidence of flowers.

JAY MACPHERSON

1931–

The Swan

White-habited, the mystic Swan
Walks her rank cloister as the night draws down,
In sweet communion with her sister shade,
Matchless and unassayed.

The tower of ivory sways,
Gaze bends to mirrored gaze:
This perfect arc embraces all her days.
And when she comes to die,
The treasures of her silence patent lie:
'I am all that is and was and shall be,
My garment may no man put by.'

The Woods no More

We'll wander to the woods no more,
Nor beat about the juniper tree.
My tears run down, my heart is sore,
And none shall make a game of me.

But come my love, another day,
I'll give you cherries with no stones,
And silver bells, and nuts in May
– But make no bones.

The Fisherman

The world was first a private park
Until the angel, after dark,
Scattered afar to wests and easts
The lovers and the friendly beasts.

And later still a home-made boat
Contained Creation set afloat,
No rift nor leak that might betray
The creatures to a hostile day.

But now beside the midnight lake
One single fisher sits awake
And casts and fights and hauls to land
A myriad forms upon the sand.

Old Adam on the naming-day
Blessed each and let it slip away:
The fisher of the fallen mind
Sees no occasion to be kind,

But on his catch proceeds to sup;
Then bends, and at one slurp sucks up
The lake and all that therein is
To slake that hungry gut of his,

Then whistling makes for home and bed
As the last morning breaks in red;
But God the Lord with patient grin
Lets down his hook and hoicks him in.

ALDEN NOWLAN

1933–

The Execution

On the night of the execution
a man at the door
mistook me for the coroner.
'Press', I said.

But he didn't understand. He led me
into the wrong room
where the sheriff greeted me:
'You're late, Padre.'

'You're wrong,' I told him. 'I'm Press.'
'Yes, of course, Reverend Press.'
We went down a stairway.

'Ah, Mr Ellis,' said the Deputy.
'Press!' I shouted. But he shoved me
through a black curtain.
The lights were so bright
I couldn't see the faces
of the men sitting
opposite. But, thank God, I thought
they can see me!

'Look!' I cried. 'Look at my face!
Doesn't anybody know me?'

Then a hood covered my head.
'Don't make it harder for us,' the hangman whispered.

Beets

Swollen to bursting like a pod, her ripeness
tense as a vegetable's (one senses
something about to snap and plop open)
the young expectant mother
gathers beets in her garden.

Their stalks and smeared leaves
could have been crushed in a wound to stanch it.
The roots themselves resemble
sickening cores hung with shredded tissue,
bloody her hands as she harvests them, absently,
her eyes unfocused, mouth half-open.

The Anatomy of Angels

Angels inhabit love songs. But they're sprites
not seraphim. The angel that up-ended
Jacob had sturdy calves, moist hairy armpits,
stout loins to serve the god whom she befriended,

and was adept at wrestling. She wore
a cobra like a girdle. Yet his bone
mending he spent some several tedious weeks
marking the bed they'd shared, with a great stone.

God Sour the Milk of the Knacking Wench

God sour the milk of the knacking wench
with razor and twine she comes
to stanchion our blond and bucking bull,
pluck out his lovely plumbs.

God shiver the prunes on her bark of chest,
who capons the prancing young.
Let maggots befoul her alive in bed,
and dibble thorns in her tongue.

LEONARD COHEN

1934–

Credo

A cloud of grasshoppers
rose from where we loved
and passed before the sun.
I wondered what farms
they would devour,
what slave people would go free
because of them.
I thought of pyramids overturned,
of Pharaoh hanging by the feet,
his body smeared –
Then my love drew me down
to conclude what I had begun.

Later, clusters of fern apart,
we lay.
A cloud of grasshoppers
passed between us and the moon,
going the other way,
each one fat and flying slow,
not hungry for the leaves and ferns
we rested on below.
The smell that burning cities give
was in the air.

Batallions of the wretched,
wild with holy promises,
soon passed our sleeping place;
they ran among
the ferns and grass.
I had two thoughts:
to leave my love
and join their wandering,

join their holiness;
        or take my love
to the city they had fled:
        That impoverished world
of boil-afflicted flesh
and rotting fields
could not tempt us from each other.

        Our ordinary morning lust
claimed my body first
and made me sane.
        I must not betray
the small oasis where we lie,
though only for a time.
        It is good to live between
a ruined house of bondage
and a holy promised land.
        A cloud of grasshoppers
will turn another Pharaoh upside-down;
slaves will build cathedrals
for other slaves to burn.
        It is good to hear
the larvae rumbling underground,
        good to learn
the feet of fierce or humble priests
trample out the green.

What I'm Doing Here

I do not know if the world has lied
I have lied
I do not know if the world has conspired against love
I have conspired against love
The atmosphere of torture is no comfort
I have tortured
Even without the mushroom cloud
still I would have hated

Listen
I would have done the same things
even if there were no death
I will not be held like a drunkard
under the cold tap of facts
I refuse the universal alibi

Like an empty telephone booth passed at night
and remembered
like mirrors in a movie palace lobby consulted
only on the way out
like a nymphomaniac who binds a thousand
into strange brotherhood
I wait
for each one of you to confess

Another Night with Telescope

Come back to me
        brutal empty room
Thin Byzantine face
        preside over this new fast
I am broken with easy grace
Let me be neither
        father nor child
but one who spins
on an eternal unimportant loom
    patterns of wars and grass
which do not last the night
        I know the stars
are wild as dust
and wait for no man's discipline
        but as they wheel
from sky to sky they rake
    our lives with pins of light

GEORGE BOWERING

1935–

Circus Maximus

They come
                    each one
of them
            a rise
like those
                  who came
before them.

New heroes flexing
to fill the shape
made out for them
by the now dead

but each new man
a refutation of his predecessor.

Camus refining Dostoyevsky
yet feeling the swell
of body the Russian felt

the old man
grizzling in his beard
anticipating the African
who would fit his fingers
over the old pen
playing with down
        on his cheek.

Who knows ten of your molecules
are not in me?

but Nature helps me define
my own shape

looks on as
I stumble over the centuries'
exposed root
lost in my own
particularity

(patterns I deny
and that
is part of a pattern).

Styles do not multiply themselves
but are all
pervasive

the suit of clothes
is nothing
without its own disfigurations.

New heroes flex into it
and bend it to their bodies.

Winter's Dregs

Thomas Hardy in the stars
a constellation looking down
look around
There is Taurus
there is the big bear
there is all the canopy
of eating & killing creatures

crowding all your greek-ending
girls
And here are we
blast-beruffled more than ever
was robin or nightingale

though now we muffle our souls
our very darkling selves ourselves

GEORGE JONAS

1935–

Five Stanzas on Perfection

I will not be reduced to what I am
For I cannot quite return to the sea.
But naked in a circle of strangers
I have only been afraid of myself.

I am a cloud: I rain for the same reason
A tree grows or a cat stalks a mouse.
A cockroach can explain nine-tenths of me.
The rest sent Buddha into the wilderness.

I may only have to cut out one very small part
To attain perfection either way.
I have been exploring myself with a knife
I can do no more for the best of my friends.

Not something simple, my limbs or my glands
(Cripples and eunuchs still have narrow lips)
Nor is it primeval selfishness alone:
I have seen women and even children weep.

But maybe an impalpable dark plane
Such as some sleep: no ripple, sight or sound
Or meeting myself very suddenly
In a little-known part of any town.

DARYL HINE

1936–

After the Agony in the Garden

At last the dawn throws the forest in relief –
the true dawn one hopes, the end of war,
coming and catching the prisoners asleep:
hope in dry hearts, sap in winter stalks –
and all the fabulary animals in their living cage,
led by a child extinguishing their grief
and like a dumb assuager giving sight
to us who sit unmoved in fields of light.

Speech is a shoot of grace
and God's minstrel and a game of heaven,
but the lord has caught this whole world
with the thin line of His love and the bait of His blood,
even the tiger in the enkindled wood
that protests the enfolding of his passion;
He lies down in each one's cenacle
to stir as if from sleep to miracle
trees seen in the inhospitable garden
where the second coming rides an enamoured world –
every page's Dominus done in gold;
after longer syllables where green and blue are hidden,
and the martyrs' bonfires indelibly red,

capitals whose lineaments are written
in parables around the story told;
He stirs His igneous limbs from each one's cold
and from his inertia makes His parables happen. . . .

Now the sun rises in a winter field
and the frozen corn stalks make a tiny wood
that marks the line between hope and Hope
resplendent upon us who sleep.

JOHN ROBERT COLOMBO

1936–

Riverdale Lion

Bound lion, almost blind from meeting their gaze and popcorn
the Saturday kids love you. It is their parents
who would paint your mane with polkadots to match their
California shirts
and would trim your nails for tieclips.

Your few roars delight them. But they wish you would quicken
your pace
and not disappear so often into your artificial cave
for there they think you partake of secret joys and race
under an African sun as gold as your mane.

But you fool them. You merely suffer the heat and scatter
the flies
with your tail. You never saw Africa.
The sign does not tell them that you were born here, in
captivity,
that you are as much a Canadian as they are.

What Pablo Picasso Did in 'Les Demoiselles d'Avignon'

He stripped five of our women
whose eyes were as open as oracles

three he broke on beds of geometry
two he placed front to back with beasts

voodoo and calculus he let loose
to corrupt our consciousness

this way he circled us into a science
this way he settled us into a savagery

LIONEL KEARNS

1937–

In-Group

No one
ran up
and shook
Christ's hand.

The only others
with that kind
of inclination

Had theirs
nailed down
too.

Insight

Christ wow
now I get
your message

It's a warning
incarnate, Man –

How this love-junk
can really
get a hold of you

How it can
hang you up
for good

TOM MARSHALL

1938–

Astrology

It's an approach. Say what you like
about it. It's an approach.
Speak of the transience of philosophies;
all are de-commissioned at last.
I admit this. It's entirely the point.

I care more about this
arrangement of words than about you.
To return one needs an approach,
'a way of happening',
and any approach will do
in a sense. The one that works
is true (of course, all are true).

Why not then take the intricate
fire of stars as way? Interlocking roses
of our summer day
are no less blasted in the tides of dust.
Why not take penmanship, ornithology?
Why not take you and me?

Can you give me of your
bare instincts enough? Save me
(though the cost may be beyond your ken)?
Do it then. For I know. But
I must know the full horoscope
of your desire. So give me
conjunctions of dust; make again
the knotted turning of the seasons start;
give me the whole fire of your heart.

JOHN NEWLOVE

1938–

I Talk to You

I talk to you (whispering and pointing
whatever it is I wish to know) and no-one
gives attention. Why should they?

The excessive sun has no intention.
It moves easily on, burning my skin.

To whom should I talk except
my exhaustive self? To whom indicate
the shape of the house I inhabit,
or the brain and the leg, the pressures
behind the bony skull, the leg's hairs,
the moulding of the front-door stairs.

To talk to myself expecting an answer,
expecting a credence, confessing
insaneness in this dialogue –

is this to be mad? To sound foolish,
to sound foolishness, to be mad to say,
to say the convulsive illegible world
is how? and demand a reply.

To be mad, to be mad, unangry, to sit
sour in the old wooden chair
and run across the unmoving world
without pity, with only the wild regret
at not to know? To be mad for an answer
knowing there is no answer, except
in peculiarities and particularities?

The chair: what sort of sunny wood
its back is made of; the leg's shape

and not the brain's. And whom to talk to:
and whether it is fit to whisper or to shout.

Good Company, Fine Houses

Good company, fine houses
and consequential people,
you will not turn me
into a tin factory.

I know where the lean and half
starved gods are hiding,
I have slept in their mountains.

I have slept among them,
in their mountains turning
nightmarishly between the rocks
and the reaching plants,

I have seen red eyes
on my throat from behind
every bush and waterfall,
greedy for blood.

Good company, fine people,
except for the shooting,
how much will your funerals cost

in your consequential houses?
I know where the god is
hiding, starved. I have slept
in the turning mountain.

GWENDOLYN MacEWEN

1941–

The Thing Is Violent

Self, I want you now to be
violent and without history,
for we've rehearsed too long our ceremonial ballet
and I fear my calm against your exquisite rage.

I do not fear that I will go mad
but that I may not, and the shadows of my sanity
blacken out your burning; act once
and you need not act again –
give me no ceremony, scars are not pain.

The thing is violent, nothing precedes it,
it has no meaning before or after –
sweet wounds which burn like stars,
stigmata of the self's own holiness,
appear and plot new zodiacs upon the flesh.

PIERRE COUPEY

1942–

Study No. X

chi ama, crede : mother
well
told me
unmaternally
for there was no sex involved (just
a
cosmos
of love) rare

in these times & spaces made of cracked-nut hearts; &
split
pea
skulls;
infanta! madonna! guernica! hiroshima!

)you are a catastrophe on the mirror of this earth
)you do not
let me
believe
(in hell
only: & it takes more courage
than red
wheelbarrows
give
to love:
flesh & dust

MICHAEL ONDAATJE

1943–

Prometheus, with wings:

They splayed him scientifically on the rock,
so that a limping sun would blind him until noon,
and crack his lips and eyelids, white his hair,
and harden blood on bitten lips and thighs.

The bird would come, peck at his puckered flesh,
lick his ribs and peel the calloused skin
until the dusk grew fat and brown
and the bird left frowning.

His crackled knuckles then released their bite
and hanging he watched sea drown half his skin
which stinging like peroxide dulled the sense
so he could grin again.

Zeus
sitting with a bunch of grapes and gods
spat out the pips
and puzzled watched this man,
who with a whitened eye and hectic lust,
wooed a host of mermaids after dusk.

Biographical Notes

ANDERSON, PATRICK: b. 1915 in England; educated at Oxford and Columbia. Came to Montreal in 1940 where he taught and was active in the 'Preview' group of writers. Taught in the University of Malaya, and is now in London, England. Has published three books of poems.

AVISON, MARGARET: b. 1918 at Galt, Ontario; educated at the University of Toronto, Guggenheim Fellow in Poetry 1956–57. Has worked at various times as secretary, librarian. Has published *Winter Sun*, 1960, and *The Dumbfounding*, 1966.

BAILEY, ALFRED G.: b. 1905 in Quebec City; educated at the Universities of New Brunswick and Toronto and at the London School of Economics and Political Science. He is Dean of Arts and Head of the Department of History at the University of New Brunswick. Has published three books of poetry, the latest *Border River*, 1952.

BIRNEY, EARLE: b. 1904 in Calgary, Alberta; educated at the Universities of British Columbia, Toronto, California, and London. Has twice won the Governor-General's Medal for poetry, was awarded a Federal Government Fellowship 1952, and the Lorne Pierce Medal of the Royal Society of Canada 1953. Now Writer-in-Residence at the University of Toronto. His *Selected Poems* appeared 1966.

BOWERING, GEORGE: b. 1935, Penticton, B.C.; educated at University of British Columbia; a founding editor of *Tish*. *Points on the Grid* appeared in 1964, *The Silver Wire*, 1966. Presently travelling after teaching at the University of Alberta.

CAMERON, GEORGE FREDERICK (1854–85): Born at New Glasgow, Nova Scotia; educated at Boston University (Law), and Queen's University. For the last three years of his life he was editor of the Kingston *News*. His selected poems, *Lyrics on Freedom, Love and Death*, appeared posthumously in 1887.

CAMPBELL, WILFRED (1858–1918): Born at Kitchener, Ontario; educated at the University of Toronto and at the Episcopal Divinity School, Cambridge, Massachusetts. Resigned from the ministry to devote himself to writing. Ran a literary column, *At the Mermaid Tavern*, in the Toronto *Globe* with Lampman and Duncan Campbell Scott. Worked in the Civil Service, Ottawa. *The Poetical Works of Wilfred Campbell* appeared in 1922.

CARMAN, BLISS (1861–1929): Born at Fredericton, New Brunswick; educated there and at the University of New Brunswick. After post-graduate work at Edinburgh and Harvard, he entered journalism in New York City. Lived for many years in New Canaan, Connecticut. Published many volumes of verse, the first, *Low Tide on Grand Pré*, appearing in 1893. The first of the three series of *Songs from Vagabondia* was written in collaboration with Richard Hovey, the Dartmouth poet. He was related to Emerson, and was a cousin of Charles G. D. Roberts. *The Selected Poems of Bliss Carman*, edited by Lorne Pierce, was published in 1954.

COHEN, LEONARD: b. 1934 in Montreal; educated at McGill University; post-graduate work at Columbia. Has published three books of verse, *Let us Compare Mythologies*, 1956, *The Spice-Box of Earth*, 1961, and *Flowers for Hitler*, 1964. Author of two novels: *The Favourite Game*, 1963, and *Beautiful Losers*, 1966.

COLOMBO, JOHN ROBERT: b. 1936 at Kitchener, Ontario; graduate of University of Toronto. Freelance writer and editor: *Poésie/Poetry 64*, *Miraculous Montages*, 1966, *Abracadabra*, 1967.

COUPEY, PIERRE: b. 1942, Montreal; attended McGill University. In Paris 1965–66 on a Quebec Government grant for poetry. Has published *Bring Forth the Cowards*, 1964. Presently in Vancouver.

CRAWFORD, ISABELLA VALANCY (1850–87): Born in Dublin, Ireland; the family migrated to Ontario when the poet was eight. Lived with her mother in Toronto in humble circumstances, writing indefatigably until her death at the age of thirty-six. The *Collected Poems* appeared in 1905.

DANIELLS, ROY: b. 1902 in London, England; educated at the University of British Columbia and Toronto University. Is Head of the Department of English at the University of British Columbia. Has published two books of poems, *Deeper into the Forest*, 1948, and *The Chequered Shade*, 1963.

DRUMMOND, WILLIAM HENRY (1854–1907): 'The Poet of the Habitant' was born near Mohill, Ireland, came with his parents to Canada while still a small boy. He attended McGill and Bishop's College, Lennoxville; established a physician's practice at Stornoway, later at Knowlton and Montreal. His *Complete Poems* was published in 1926.

DUDEK, LOUIS: b. 1918 in Montreal; educated at McGill and Columbia. On the Faculty of English, McGill University. Was a partner in Contact Press, Toronto, and editor of *Delta* and the

... seven books of poetry, the ... *Mêxico*, 1958.

...a, Ontario; is head of a public- ... published books are *Three Dozen* ... *Momos*, 1958, *Blind Man's Holiday*, ... *Angel*, 1965.

... in Freeport, Long Island; educated at ... onto and the Sorbonne. Is Professor of ... sity of Toronto. Has published *Poems*, ... *of the Hills*, 1948, *Acis in Oxford* and *Dover Be...* 1961, and *The Silverthorn Bush*, 1966.

FORD, R...: b. 1915 in Ottawa; educated at the University of Western Ontario and Cornell. Member of the Department of External Affairs. Is at present Canadian Ambassador to The Soviet Union. His book of poems, *A Window on the North*, was published in 1956.

GLASSCO, JOHN: b. 1909 in Montreal and educated at McGill University; poet, translator, and expert horseman, resident in the Eastern Townships. Has published two books of poetry, *The Deficit Made Flesh*, 1958, and *A Point of Sky*, 1964. Has translated *The Journal of Saint-Denys-Garneau*, 1962, and edited *English Poetry in Quebec*, 1965.

GOLDSMITH, OLIVER (1794–1861): Canada's first native-born poet in English, born at St Andrew's, New Brunswick. Entered Government service and became Deputy Commissary General, serving in Canada and abroad. He was a grandnephew of the author of *The Deserted Village*, the prototype for *The Rising Village*. The second edition of *The Rising Village*, with shorter poems, was published in 1834.

GRIER, ELDON: b. 1917 of Canadian parentage in London, England; educated in Montreal. Taught painting at the Montreal Museum of Fine Arts. Is the author of four books of poems. *A Morning from Scraps*, Spain 1955, *Poems*, 1956, *The Ring of Ice*, 1957, and *A Friction of Lights*, 1963.

GUSTAFSON, RALPH: b. 1909 in Lime Ridge, Quebec; educated at Bishop's University and Oxford. Author of four volumes of poetry, the latest, *Sift in an Hourglass*, 1966. Besides the present book, has edited two others in the Penguin series, *Anthology of Canadian Poetry*, 1942, and *Canadian Accent*, 1944; and *Canadian Poets*, New Directions, 1943. Professor and Poet-in-Residence at Bishop's University.

BIOGRAPHICAL NOTES

HEAVYSEGE, CHARLES (1816–76): born in Huddersfield, England, came to Montreal in 1853 where he worked as a cabinet-maker and carpenter, and in journalism. *Saul: A Drama in Three Parts* appeared in 1857, and revised, in 1869; this was followed by *Count Filippo; or The Unequal Marriage*, 1860, and five other volumes of verse. (The sections here given are to be found as follows: Malzah's soliloquy in the grounds of Saul's palace, Third Part, Act I, sc. V. Saul's soliloquies at Endor and the Hebrew Camps, Third Part, Act VI, sc. VIII, X, XI. The selection from *Count Filippo* is from Act IV, sc. VII. The Song from *Count Filippo* occurs in Act II, sc. V.)

HERBIN, JOHN FREDERIC (1860–1923): born in Windsor, Nova Scotia; educated at Acadia University. Lived as a jeweller in Wolfville, N.S. His books of poems are *Canada and Other Poems*, 1891; and *The Marshlands*, 1899.

HINE, DARYL: b. 1936 in Vancouver; educated at McGill University. Has published *Five Poems*, 1954, *The Carnal and the Crane*, 1957, *The Devil's Picture Book*, 1960, and *The Wooden Horse*, 1965.

JOHNSTON, GEORGE: b. 1913 Hamilton, Ontario; educated at University of Toronto; now professor of English at Carleton University in Ottawa. Has published *The Cruising Auk*, 1959, and *Home Free*, 1966.

JONAS, GEORGE: b. 1935 in Budapest, Hungary. Since 1957 has lived in Toronto where he works as editor for the C.B.C. A selection of his poetry appeared in Souster's *New Wave Canada*, 1966.

JONES, D. G.: b. 1929 at Bancroft, Ontario; educated at McGill and Queen's Universities. Professor at Sherbrooke University. Has published *Frost on the Sun*, 1957, *The Sun is Axeman*, 1961, and *Phrases from Orpheus*, 1967.

KEARNS, LIONEL: b. 1937 in Nelson, B.C., and educated at the University of British Columbia; presently in the Department of English at Simon Fraser University. Has published *Songs of Circumstance*, 1963, and *Listen George*, 1965.

KENNEDY, LEO: b. 1907 in Liverpool, England, brought to Canada at the age of five; educated in Montreal. Was associated with the *McGill Fortnightly Review* and the *Canadian Mercury*. Now living in the United States as an advertising writer. Has published one book of poems, *The Shrouding*, 1933.

KLEIN, A. M.: b. 1909 in Montreal; educated at McGill University and at the University of Montreal. Editor, Visiting Lecturer in Poetry at McGill, 1945–48, he is a barrister by profession, living in Montreal. He has published four books of poems, *Hath not a Jew* ... 1940, *The Hitleriad*, 1944, *Poems*, 1944, *The Rocking Chair and Other Poems*, winner of the Governor-General's Award, 1948, and a novel, *The Second Scroll*, 1951.

KNISTER, RAYMOND (1899–1932): Born near Comber, Ontario; worked on his father's farm near Blenheim, and attended Victoria College, Toronto. Was on the staff of *The Midland* in the United States, then returned to Toronto, freelance writing. His premature death was by drowning. Author of two novels, *White Narcissus*, 1929, and *My Star Predominant*, which appeared in 1934, and editor of *Canadian Short Stories*, 1928. His *Collected Poems* was published in 1949.

LAMPMAN, ARCHIBALD (1861–99): Born at Morpeth, Ontario, and educated at Trinity College, Toronto. From 1883 on he was in the Post Office Department of the Civil Service, Ottawa. His first book was *Among the Millet*, 1888, this was followed by *Lyrics of Earth*, 1895. His selected poems, *Lyrics of Earth*, appeared in 1925 edited, with an introduction by his friend, Duncan Campbell Scott, who was also joint editor with E. K. Brown of *At the Long Sault*, 1943, a selection from Lampman's unpublished manuscripts. *Selected Poems*, from the whole of Lampman's work, edited, with a memoir by Duncan Campbell Scott, appeared in 1947.

LANIGAN, GEORGE T. (1846–86): Born at Three Rivers, Quebec. Founded the newspaper that is now the *Montreal Star*, and did newspaper work in the United States, Lanigan wrote his fables, published under the title, *Fables Out of the World*, in 1887, for the *New York World*.

LAYTON, IRVING: b. 1912 in Rumania and came as an infant with his parents to Montreal; educated at McGill University; active in the literary First Statement group, publishing his first book of poems, *Here and Now*, in 1945. Many subsequent volumes culminated in his *Collected Poems*, 1965. Lectures at Sir George Williams University in Montreal. Editor of *Love Where the Nights are Long*, 1962.

LE PAN, DOUGLAS: b. 1914 in Toronto; educated at the University of Toronto and Oxford. Joined the Department of External Affairs; was Professor of English at Queen's University; now Principal of University College in the University of Toronto. Has published two books of poems, *The Wounded Prince*, 1948, and *The Net and the Sword*, 1953; and a novel, *The Deserter*, 1964.

LESLIE, KENNETH: b. 1892 at Pictou, Nova Scotia; educated at Dalhousie, Nebraska, and Harvard universities. Formerly editor of the *Protestant*. Has published four books of poems, the latest, *By Stubborn Stars*, winner of the Governor-General's Award 1938.

LIVESAY, DOROTHY: b. 1909 in Winnipeg; educated at the University of Toronto and the Sorbonne. Did social work in Montreal, Vancouver, and with UNESCO in Northern Rhodesia. Lecturer in poetry at the Universities of British Columbia and New Brunswick. Her *Selected Poems* appeared in 1957; *The Colour of God's Face* in 1964, *The Unquiet Bed*, 1967.

LOWRY, MALCOLM: (1909–57). Born in Merseyside, England; educated at Cambridge. Spent several years at sea; in British Columbia; and again in England. Author of the novels, *Ultramarine*, 1933, and *Under the Volcano*, 1947, and a book of stories, *Hear Us O Lord from Heaven Thy Dwelling Place*, 1961. His *Selected Poems*, edited by Earle Birney, appeared in 1962.

MACEWEN, GWENDOLYN: b. Toronto in 1941; left school to devote herself to a literary career. Her book of poems, *The Rising Fire*, was published in 1963; *A Breakfast for Barbarians* in 1966; a novel, *Julian, the Magician*, 1963.

MACINNES, TOM (1867–1951): Born at Dresden, Ontario: educated at the University of Toronto; called to the bar, 1893. Drafted the Canadian Immigration Act; travelled extensively in the Canadian Northwest and in China. His *Complete Poems*, 1923, was followed by *High Low Along*, 1934, *Rhymes of a Rounder*, Vancouver 1935, and *In the Old of my Age*, 1947.

MACKAY, L. A.: b. 1901 at Hensall, Ontario; educated at the University of Toronto and at Oxford; Guggenheim Fellow 1945; Taught at the universities of Toronto and British Columbia; now Professor of Latin at the University of California. Has published two books of poems, *Viper's Bugloss*, 1938, and *The Ill-Tempered Lover*, 1948.

MACPHERSON, JAY: b. 1931, in England; educated at Carleton College, Ottawa, and the University of Toronto, where she now lectures. Has published three books of poems, *Nineteen Poems*, 1952, *O Earth Return*, 1954, and *The Boatman*, 1957.

MAIR, CHARLES (1838–1927): Born at Lanark, Ontario; educated at Queen's University. One of the originators of the 'Canada First' movement; took part in the suppression of both Riel rebellions; member on government expeditions into British Columbia, and of the Immigration Department. *Dreamland and Other Poems* appeared in 1868, and *Tecumseh: A Drama* in 1886.

MANDEL, E. W.: b. 1922 in Estevan, Saskatchewan; educated at the universities of Saskatchewan and Toronto. Now professor in the English Department at University of Alberta. Has published *Fuseli Poems*, 1960, *Black and Secret Man*, 1964, and *An Idiot Joy*, 1967.

MARSHALL, TOM: b. 1938 at Niagara Falls; educated at Queen's University and University of London. A selection of his poems appeared in *The Beast with Three Backs*, Quarry Press, 1965.

MCCRAE, JOHN (1872–1918): Born in Guelph, Ontario: educated at the University of Toronto. Served in the South African War, in Montreal hospitals, and as a medical officer in the First World War. *In Flanders Fields* first appeared in *Punch*, 8 December, 1915. His collected poems, *In Flanders Fields*, appeared in 1918.

MCLACHLAN, ALEXANDER (1818–96): Born near Glasgow; came to Ontario in 1840, where he established himself as a farmer, first on his one-acre lot at Erin, and later at Amaranth. Lectured in Britain in 1863 on the advantages of immigrating to Canada. *The Poetical Works of Alexander McLachlan* was published in 1900.

NEWLOVE, JOHN: b. Regina, Saskatchewan, 1938; attended University of Saskatchewan; now living in Vancouver. A collection of his poems, *Moving in Alone*, was published by Contact Press in 1965.

NOWLAN, ALDEN: b. Windsor, Nova Scotia, 1933; news editor of *The Telegraph-Journal* in Saint John, New Brunswick. Has published five books of poetry, the latest being *The Things which Are*, 1962.

ONDAATJE, MICHAEL: b. 1943 in Ceylon; educated in Canada at Bishop's University and University of Toronto; presently doing graduate work at Queen's. One book of poems, *The Dainty Monsters*, The Coach House Press, 1967.

PAGE, P. K.: b. 1916 in England; educated at St Hilda's School, Calgary. Was a member of the 'Preview' group in Montreal, worked for the Film Board, Ottawa. Has published *As Ten, as Twenty*, 1946, and *The Metal and the Flower*, 1954.

PICKTHALL, MARJORIE (1883–1922): Born in Gunnersbury, England; educated at Bishop Strachan School, Toronto. From 1913 to 1920 she lived in England, subsequently in British Columbia. She wrote two novels, and a book of short stories, *Angels'*

Shoes, 1923. *The Complete Poems of Marjorie Pickthall* was published in 1936.

PRATT, E. J.: (1883–1964) b. at Western Bay, Newfoundland; educated at Methodist College, St John's, and at the University of Toronto. The recipient of many honours, a C.M.G., and three times winner of the Governor-General's Award for poetry. Until his retirement in 1953, taught English at the University of Toronto. His *Collected Poems* appeared in 1958.

PURDY, ALFRED: b. 1918 near Wooler, Ontario; attended Albert College; lives at Ameliasburg, Ontario. His recent books are *Poems for All the Annettes*, 1962, *The Blur in Between*, 1963, *The Cariboo Horses*, 1965, and *North of Summer*, poems from Baffin Island, 1967.

REANEY, JAMES: b. 1926 at Stratford, Ontario; educated at the University of Toronto; teaches literature at the University of Western Ontario and edits the magazine *Alphabet*. Has published *The Red Heart*, 1949, *A Suit of Nettles*, 1957, *Twelve Letters to a Small Town*, 1962, and *The Killdeer and Other Plays*, 1962.

ROBERTS, SIR CHARLES G. D. (1860–1943): Born at Douglas, New Brunswick; educated at Fredericton Grammar School and at the University of New Brunswick. After teaching in Canada, spent many years in the United States and England. From 1925 on, lived in Toronto. Achieved an international reputation as a poet, and for his nature stories. *Selected Poems*, edited by Desmond Pacey, was published in 1955.

ROBERTS, THEODORE GOODRIDGE (1877–1953): Born in Fredericton, New Brunswick, brother of Sir Charles G. D. Roberts; educated at the University of New Brunswick. Author of a number of novels and romances of adventure. *The Leather Bottle*, a volume of selected verse, appeared in 1924.

ROSS, W. W. E.: (1894–1966) b. at Peterborough, Ontario; educated at the University of Toronto. Geophysicist with the Agincourt Magnetic Observatory near Toronto. Has published *Laconics*, 1930, *Sonnets*, 1932, and *Experiment*, 1956.

SANGSTER, CHARLES (1822–93): Born at Kingston, Ontario, where he had his schooling. Entered journalism, and then, in 1867, the Civil Service, Ottawa. Published two volumes of poetry, *The St Lawrence and the Saguenay and Other Poems*, 1856, and *Hesperus and Other Poems and Lyrics*, 1860. (The stanzas selected from 'The St Lawrence and the Saguenay' are XI–XIII, XXXI, and LXVI.)

SCOTT, DUNCAN CAMPBELL (1862–1947): Born in Ottawa: educated at Stanstead College, Quebec, and the University of Toronto. Had a long and distinguished career in the Department of Indian Affairs, retiring in 1932. Author of two volumes of short stories, *In the Village of Viger*, 1896, re-issued 1945, and *The Witching of Elspie*, 1923. His *Collected Poems* was published in 1926, *The Green Cloister*, 1935, *The Circle of Affection*, containing both prose and verse, 1947, and *Selected poems*, edited by E. K. Brown, 1951.

SCOTT, FREDERICK GEORGE (1861–1944): Born in Montreal; educated at Bishop's University and King's College, London. From 1925 Archdeacon of Quebec. Served in the First World War as senior chaplain, 1st Canadian Division, and wrote *The Great War as I Saw It*, 1922. His collected *Poems* appeared in 1936.

SCOTT, F. R.: b. 1899 in Quebec City, son of Archdeacon Scott; educated at Bishop's University, at Oxford, and McGill. Was Dean of the Faculty of Law at McGill; U.N. representative in Burma; now a member of the Royal Commission on Biculturalism and Bilingualism. Has written widely on national and international affairs. Co-editor of the anthology, *New Provinces*, 1936, and member of the 'Preview' group of poets in Montreal. His *Selected Poems* appeared in 1966. Co-editor of *The Blasted Pine*, 1957.

SHEARD, VIRNA (d. 1943): Born in Cobourg, Ontario; educated there and in Toronto. Author of several books of fiction, for children and adults; her selected poems, *Leaves in the Wind*, appeared in 1938.

SMITH, A. J. M.: b. 1902 in Montreal; educated at McGill University and Edinburgh. Professor of English at Michigan State University. Guggenheim Fellow, editor and critic of Canadian literature. Has edited *The Book of Canadian Poetry*, 1943, 1948, and 1957, *Seven Centuries of Verse*, 1946, *The Worldly Muse*, 1951, *The Blasted Pine*, with F. R. Scott, 1957, *The Oxford Book of Canadian Verse*, 1958, 1966, *A Book of Modern Canadian Verse*, 1967; and *The Book of Canadian Prose*, 1965. His *Collected Poems* appeared in 1962.

SMITH, KAY: b. 1911 in Saint John, New Brunswick; educated at Mount Allison University. Teaches English and dramatics in the Saint John Vocational School. Author of *Footnote to the Lord's Prayer and Other Poems*, 1951.

SOUSTER, RAYMOND: b. 1921 in Toronto where he was educated and is an accountant. Was editor of Contact Press, a non-profit organization promoting modern Canadian poetry, and of an anthology, *New Wave Canada*, 1966, presenting and stimulating the work of seventeen young writers. His collected poetry, *The Colour of the Times*, appeared in 1964; *Ten Elephants on Yonge Street* in 1965.

WADDINGTON, MIRIAM: b. 1917 in Winnipeg; educated at the Universities of Toronto and Pennsylvania; now in the Department of English at York University in Toronto. Has published four books of poetry, *Green World*, 1945, *The Second Silence*, 1955, *The Season's Lovers*, 1958, and *The Glass Trumpet*, 1966.

WARR, BERTRAM (1917–43): b. 1917 in Toronto; educated there. Lived in London; joined R.A.F. in 1941; killed in action 1943. Published Broadsheet No. 3, *Yet a Little Onwards*, in Resurgam Younger Poets, Favil Press, 1941.

WATSON, WILFRED: b. 1911 in Rochester, England; came to Canada in 1925; educated at the University of British Columbia and Toronto. Professor of English at the University of Alberta. Has published one book of poetry, *Friday's Child*, 1955.

WEBB, PHYLLIS: b. 1927 in Victoria, British Columbia; educated at the University of British Columbia and at McGill. Has published *Even Your Right Eye*, 1956, *The Sea is Also a Garden*, 1962, and *Naked Poems*, 1965.

WILKINSON, ANNE (1910–1961): b. in Toronto; had informal education, mostly in schools abroad. Was an editor of *The Tamarack Review*. Published a history of the Osler family, *Lions in the Way*, 1956, and two books of poetry, *Counterpoint to Sleep*, 1951, and *The Hangman Ties the Holly*, 1955.

Index of Titles

Index of Authors

MORE ABOUT PENGUINS

If you have enjoyed reading this book you may wish to know that *Penguin Book News* appears every month. It is an attractively illustrated magazine containing a complete list of books published by Penguins and still in print, together with details of the month's new books. A specimen copy will be sent free on request.

Penguin Book News is obtainable from most bookshops; but you may prefer to become a regular subscriber at 3s. for twelve issues. Just write to Dept EP, Penguin Books Ltd, Harmondsworth, Middlesex, enclosing a cheque or postal order, and you will be put on the mailing list.

Some other books published by Penguins are described on the following pages.

Note : *Penguin Book News* is not available in the U.S.A., Canada or Australia

THE PENGUIN BOOK OF SPANISH VERSE

Edited by J. M. Cohen

No body of lyrical poetry is so seriously underestimated by English readers as the Spanish. For the majority, Spain is the country of a single prose masterpiece, *Don Quixote*, and of a dramatic literature much praised at home, which has, however, never been successfully translated, let alone presented on the British stage; Lope de Vega, Tirso de Molina, Pedro Calderón de la Barca are no more than names to those who have not read them in the original. So, indeed, are the Spanish lyrical poets, though with the added disadvantage that here Spain has not the reputation of France or Italy. Nevertheless, during her two grand periods she was certainly the equal, and possibly the superior, of either in this field. These two great flowerings of Spanish poetry, to which this anthology is devoted, lasted, the first for upwards of two centuries, from the beginning of the fifteenth to halfway through the seventeenth, and the second for some fifty years, from the 1880s to the defeat of the Spanish Republic in the Civil War.

In this collection the Spanish poems are accompanied by English prose translations.

THE PENGUIN BOOK OF FRENCH VERSE

(This collection contains a plain prose translation of each poem)

VOLUME I

To the Fifteenth Century

EDITED BY BRIAN WOLEDGE

This volume covers the earliest six hundred years of French poetry. It contains an excellent selection of verse, much of it naturally anonymous, stretching from the *Chanson de Roland* to the work of François Villon.

VOLUME 2

The Sixteenth to the Eighteenth Century

EDITED BY GEOFFREY BRERETON

A selection from 46 poets covering nearly three hundred years of French poetry, from the decline of the medieval influence to the beginnings of Romanticism, including French verse of the Renaissance. Considerable space has been given to the 'irregulars' of the earlier half of the period and the 'baroque' poets are for the first time placed in perspective.

VOLUME 3

The Nineteenth Century

EDITED BY ANTHONY HARTLEY

This century, which includes such names as Baudelaire, Hugo, Rimbaud, and Mallarmé, can rank with the greatest eras of world literature. The poems included have been chosen on their merits and not merely to illustrate historical development.

VOLUME 4

The Twentieth Century

EDITED BY ANTHONY HARTLEY

An introduction to this volume analyses the relationship between modern French verse and English and European literature, and the collection extends from the turn of the century to the present day. it includes Claudel, Valéry, Péguy, Aragon, and many others.

WRITING TODAY

A new series of contemporary world literature is now being published in Penguins. It aims to bridge the cultural gaps imposed by language and distance with selections in English of the work of the best writers and poets of other lands.

Other books in the series on sale or in preparation

AFRICAN WRITING TODAY
ITALIAN WRITING TODAY
GERMAN WRITING TODAY
LATIN AMERICAN WRITING TODAY
SOUTH AFRICAN WRITING TODAY
*THE NEW WRITING IN THE U.S.A.
POLISH WRITING TODAY
FRENCH WRITING TODAY

* NOT FOR SALE IN THE U.S.A

CONTEMPORARY AMERICAN POETRY

Donald Hall

This book is a counterpart to *Modern American Verse* by Geoffrey Moore, although it is more personal in its selection than our previous book. Donald Hall, well-known as poet and critic both here and in America, has catholic taste, and has steered his course between the extravagances of the 'beat' poets and the cautious academic verse turned out by the products of the departments of creative writing. Aware both of the dangers of American literature becoming a suburb of English literature, and of it getting too idiomatic in protest against the Eliot-Auden influence, he has included both the 'European Americans' and the more national followers of William Carlos Williams who stayed at home. No poet is included who published a book before 1946, so the collection is literally of post-war American poetry, with twenty-five poets and 130 poems. Among those included are W. D. Snodgrass, who won the Guinness prize in London, and Merwin, Wilbur, and Lowell, who are all well-known in this country.